# the
# flight
# instructor's
# survival
# guide

# the flight instructor's survival guide

true, witty, insightful stories illustrating the fundamentals of instructing

## Arlynn McMahon

**Aviation Supplies & Academics, Inc.**
Newcastle, Washington

*The Flight Instructor's Survival Guide: True, Witty, Insightful Stories Illustrating the Fundamentals of Instructing*
by Arlynn McMahon

Aviation Supplies & Academics, Inc.
7005 132nd Place SE
Newcastle, Washington 98059-3153
asa@asa2fly.com | asa2fly.com

© 2017 Aviation Supplies & Academics, Inc.

**ASA-CFI-SG**
ISBN 978-1-61954-429-1

Printed in the United States of America
2021   2020   2019   2018          9   8   7   6   5   4   3   2

*Library of Congress Cataloging-in-Publication Data*
Names: McMahon, Arlynn, author.
Title: The flight instructor's survival guide : true, witty, insightful stories illus-
    trating the fundamentals of instructing / by Arlynn McMahon.
Description: Newcastle, WA : Aviation Supplies & Academics, Inc., [2017]
Identifiers: LCCN 2016024957 | ISBN 9781619544291 (trade paper) | ISBN
    1619544296 (trade paper)
Subjects: LCSH: Flight training—Study and teaching—United States. | Air
    pilots—Training of—Psychological aspects. | Air pilots—Training of—Case
    studies. | Educational psychology.
Classification: LCC TL712 .M393 2016 | DDC 629.132/52—dc23
LC record available at https://lccn.loc.gov/2016024957

# contents

# disclaimer

The methods and opinions in this book are that of its author. Every training situation is different and the advice or strategies contained herein may not be suitable for you. You are advised to work with an experienced qualified certificated flight instructor.

# foreword
## by rod machado

An old Chinese aphorism suggests that it is better to spend three years looking for a good instructor than to spend even three minutes with a bad one. If you were lucky, the first flight instructor you found was a good one. If fortune smiled on you, however, and all relevant celestial bodies were properly aligned, you found Arlynn McMahon.

Four and a half decades in the aviation business have exposed me to many amazing flight instructors, and Arlynn is one of the best I've seen. She's highly skilled, capable, and competent, without question. Her signature contribution in the aviation community, however, is the rarest of all cockpit qualities. I'm speaking of *wisdom*—the wisdom that Arlynn brings to each flight training session. It's a quality that's fundamental to producing safe pilots, and it comes from her deep understanding of human nature.

*The Flight Instructor's Survival Guide* is more than a book about flight instructing. It's a book about human nature as it is reflected in the cockpit. Within its pages are forty-four powerful instructional stories about students of all levels who struggle to master the unknown—the environment, the airplane, but mostly their own human nature. Arlynn understands this struggle and skillfully applies her tradecraft to make the flight training experience a meaningful one.

Arlynn can do this because she's part psychologist, part philosopher, part mom, and even part lawman. She's adept and intellectually flexible enough to assume any and all identities as the flight training situation demands. Wielding her training aids, writing board, and eraser with masterful intent, she effectively dismantles her student's anxiety, self-doubt, and confusion. In their place, she creates the opportunity for her students to learn something new. In the process, they become something new.

That's why *The Flight Instructor's Survival Guide* is an excellent book for flight instructors. It begins where the FAA's *Aviation Instructor's Handbook* ends. It presents practical advice—by way of concrete examples, no less—on ethics, character, and professional values. Arlynn shows us how to handle some of the most difficult and challenging dilemmas that all flight instructors face at one time or another. She demonstrates how to do this smartly, with grace, style, and wisdom. Any instructor or instructor applicant (or pilot, for that matter) worth his or her weight in slow-running Hobbs meters is advised to read this book—and to read it more than once.

In the 1970s, ten of the nation's top martial arts masters were asked the following question: *If you only had one hour to spend with a student, what technique would you teach that person?* In every instance, each martial arts master said that he wouldn't teach any technique; instead, he would discuss the philosophy of his art with that student.

While we might not be fortunate enough to fly with Arlynn and hear her philosophy of flight training firsthand, we can spend an hour (or several) with her by reading *The Flight Instructor's Survival Guide*. Do this, and you'll be spending time with a true master of aviation instruction.

Rod Machado
San Clemente, CA
March 21, 2016

# acknowledgments

"I'm writing a book about my customers in flight training."

"Oh God, <gulp> am I in it?"

"Uh, should you be?"

"Yeah, do you remember that time when I…. Boy, that was a doozy. Someone could really learn from my mistake!"

That's the way they viewed it. When I called clients to tell them what I was doing, they each saw it as a badge of honor. They were happy to know that their story—sharing their experience—could perhaps lessen another pilot's pain.

I'd like to thank all the customers who have allowed me the honor of sharing their lives and cockpits through the years and especially those included in this book.

# introduction

The FAA *Aviation Instructor's Handbook* (AIH, FAA-H-8083-9) is required reading and is the reference for the Fundamentals of Instructing (FOI) FAA Knowledge Exam—a required test for all ground and flight instructors. The AIH is not an aviation book but a text that details human behavior and communication; it's the basis for how flight instructors teach and how students learn. Psychology is a thick portion of many chapters.

Educational psychology, better known as the fundamentals of instructing, is a foreign subject to most pilots. Because the fundamentals appear to have little to do with flying, the aspiring instructor is not excited by the concepts. The inclination is to memorize clinical-sounding terminology and make up acronyms as memory joggers for passing the test. On top of that, recent revisions to the AIH have added more bulk to theoretical concepts, at the expense of any practical how-to. What is missing is someone who can show *how* fundamentals of instructing concepts fit into the job of a flight instructor.

In teaching ground schools for instructor applicants, I find it helpful to share with students my experiences with prior clients. These stories help to illustrate how the fundamentals of instructing have applied to my job of making safe pilots. Stories usually include a bit of commentary—something that goes beyond the text, but is relevant to the job of a flight instructor.

*The Flight Instructor's Survival Guide* is a collection of short stories that I tell while teaching ground school. They've been collected over a span of 30 years and 10,000 hours of dual given.

These narratives graphically emphasize important concepts from the AIH. The fundamentals of instructing apply to each of us, not as pilots or instructors, but as humans. There is a piece of each of us in these tales. You might find yourself relating to these students and their challenges—or to me, at times, a bewildered instructor.

Real clients and events inspired the stories in this book. Of course, I've told them from my memory and from the perspective of a flight instructor, and yes, I changed identifying details to maintain their anonymity.

I tell some of these stories from the perspective of a new instructor, while others reflect me as a chief instructor and school administrator. Sometimes the "student" is actually an instructor that I supervised or mentored.

This book is a necessary companion to the AIH for anyone desiring to develop aviation-citizens with character, professionalism, and ethical values.

Throughout the book, I have referred to generic students and customers as "he." It certainly doesn't leave out the feminine; it's just easier to read. In fact, you'll notice that a good many of my clients are female.

# 1

stories
about
## human behavior

Maslow doesn't get enough credit.

If trouble is brewing with a student, look first to Maslow to fix it. Maslow is with us every day—people have to eat several times and it's just as important to have other needs met numerous times each day. Chances are good that the student's problem is rooted in basic needs.

Let's assume you've just finished the flight portion of a lesson and now you're headed back to the classroom. Instead of rushing the student through the debrief, try something different. Say something like, "Take a quick break, get a drink and I'll meet you in the classroom when you're ready." After the client has returned, inquire, "Were there any aircraft discrepancies that we should write up?" And, if you should pass another student on the way to document the discrepancies, introduce everyone. Can you see how we're meeting basic needs?

Only after the student's first three levels of basic needs are met is he fully prepared to learn. But, don't stop there. Find opportunities to reassure him that you believe he has the right stuff. Give him a few small windmills to conquer and remind him that something very worthwhile is just over his horizon. Now you've pulled him up a little higher on his pyramid.

**Figure 1-1.** Maslow's Hierarchy of Needs. (FAA)

In this chapter, you'll meet a few clients whose basic needs were obvious, a few that were not, and some whose needs I failed to meet.

# Walter

At 40-something, he still possessed the chiseled body of an athlete who played hard. Everything about Walter's life was big. He had a prosperous private medical practice, a big beautiful family, and a big house, and hewas already talking about buying a big hanger for his first plane.

During our flight training, Walter completed every assignment effortlessly. I could have soloed him in eight hours—he was that good. Still, I waited until hour twelve, just because. He scored 100 percent on his Private Pilot Knowledge Exam and in that way, he was a challenging student.

It bothered me that I had never seen Walter make a mistake. He never bounced a landing. He never needed a go-around, never got lost or tongue-tied while speaking to ATC. He was always sure of himself.

I never had the opportunity to see him correct a mistake or handle a bad situation and it bothered me that I didn't have a clue about how he might react.

Then it happened.

It was the last leg of our dual cross-country. Everything was perfect. The VOR needle was straight up. Every ETA was recorded and each checkpoint accounted for. He had even pre-set the KLEX ATIS into the standby frequency on the #1 COM, just waiting for the miles to click away. I asked what *should* have been a simple question: "How many miles is it from our current position to Lexington?"

He confidently snapped the plastic plotter down on the sectional in his lap and pronounced, "102 miles." *Hummm…*that's not right, I thought to myself. And, so, there it was—the first and only Walter-mistake. It was the tiny mistake of reading a WAC scale against a sectional chart. Everyone's done it.

I wanted him to work through it. I wanted him to find his own mistake without me pointing at it. Alternately, I wanted him to consider suitable options based on his *perceived* information. "That doesn't sound right," I inquired, "how many miles is this entire leg?" After he incorrectly read the WAC mileage for the second time, I asked if that was the number that he recorded on the NavLog during our planning.

"No, it's not!" Deep furrows formed into his forehead, marking his confusion. I could almost hear his blood pressure rising. "Sixty miles are missing from my planning computations."

My goal was to get him thinking out ahead of our current position; I wanted his thinking to project ahead of the plane. "Well, how will the additional mileage affect our fuel supply in reaching Lexington?"

He expertly whizzed the manual E6B through a few rotations before the realization hit, "We don't have enough fuel! We can't make Lexington!" His eyes were large. He was horrified.

I pressed further, "OK, what are we going to do about it?"

"What are *we* going to do about it?" His voice increased in volume with the overemphasis on *we*. "*We* aren't going to do anything. *You* fix this," and with that, he defiantly removed his hand from the C152's controls and folded his arms across his chest. The plane, without autopilot, flew on trim and stability alone.

"You do realize," his tone now matter-of-fact, "this is all *your* fault. Yeah, you're the instructor. *You* looked over my planning. *You* were supposed to be checking my work. *You* should have caught this. I did a hundred calculations. I can't be expected to get every one perfect."

While I was considering how to respond, he continued, "This is not my fault. You kept pushing me '...update the weather, preflight the plane, come on, we gotta get out of here,'" his voice mocking mine. "You are the worst instructor ever. I don't know why I chose you. You should have fixed this before we even got in this plane."

My head was reeling; I was confused. Then suddenly he began thinking ahead—far, far ahead.

"Oh no! If I die today, my wife will have to raise five little boys all by herself. Oh geez, I don't have enough life insurance. She'll lose the house. Oh my God! The boys' college fund—I haven't even set that up yet." He was becoming hysterical.

I was shell-shocked. Maybe that's why it took longer than it should have to recognize his defense mechanisms. I remembered reading about them during flight instructor training. I just saw resignation when he crossed his arms. I recognized compensation, rationalization, projection, displacement and denial. OK, once I understood what was happening, it was time to get to work.

"Walter, please fly the plane."

"No!"

"We need to make a plan, let's work together. I'll fly. You have the chart; you navigate. Is there an airport nearby that we can divert to?"

Without modern avionics, he had only the sectional to assess our surroundings. "Yes, we should be able to make Danville," his voice now hopeful. He got to work plotting a heading and took the flight controls.

Once it appeared that we were safe, he calmed down some but he wasn't finished chastising me. He was patronizing through the entire 25 very long miles to Danville. My young 20-something years of age made me open to his fatherly-type reprimanding of my teaching technique. I didn't utter a word. He suggested several improvements to my supervision abilities. He offered 101 ways to improve the way I looked, the way I talked and even the way I wrote in his logbook. Nothing about me escaped his ridicule. I sat quietly and continued to watch the sky for traffic.

We must have had a horrific headwind for the eternity that passed while en route to Danville. By the time he was preparing for descent to traffic pattern altitude, I had had more than enough. "Ooo-kay, fly heading 030. Take me to Lexington." I added a pointing palm toward my new destination to emphasize the direction.

His face was perplexed. A suddenly confident, commanding voice suggested I knew something he didn't. "You made a mistake," I tried to sound unthreatening and reassuring, "We are fine. We have plenty of fuel to make Lexington. Just please, take me home." Surprisingly, he was quick to become calm and compliant.

The remainder of the flight was without a word. He managed every task perfectly including a flawless landing. Returned to the ramp, he retarded the mixture and exited the plane. He didn't tie her down. He didn't collect his flight bag. He hustled through the flight school office without saying goodbye to anyone. The wheels on the big Mercedes squealed as he departed the parking lot.

*Bingo!* Escaping his problem, Walter just scored 100 percent on defense mechanisms.

Left alone to secure the plane, I felt empty and sad about how the situation had turned. A wonderful cross-country on a beautiful day had somehow twisted to bad. I called my mentor, Charlie, for some advice and encouraging words. He was pretty clear that I handled Walter all wrong. I should have diffused him earlier. By allowing the situation to worsen, it ignited out of control. It's very likely that now Walter's ego was shattered and he would be too embarrassed to show his face around the airport.

At the time, with probably 100 hours of dual instruction, I had never before seen defense mechanisms—at least not like that. I was totally unprepared for how sudden they might come on or how explosive they could be. Somehow, I was under the assumption that a student would lean to a single one or the other for defense. No one ever told me that a student could fire all the defense mechanisms and all at once—simultaneously and sequentially. Trapped in the smallness of a cockpit, there is no cover for an unsuspecting instructor.

It was good that I had learned about defense mechanisms during instructor training. Once it dawned on me what was going on with Walter, it helped me to deflect his verbal attacks. Without this knowledge, when Walter started his assault, I might have been inclined to defend myself—and *my* defense mechanisms might have flared. Then we would have been two people focused on winning the fight rather than on piloting the plane. It was a big learning day for me.

After several heartfelt apologies and much groveling on my part, Walter eventually agreed to a truce but our relationship was never the same. He completed training and passed his Private Pilot Practical Exam on the first attempt…of course. Unfortunately, I never saw him again after the final handshake and graduation photo. It wasn't my choice; I think he was uncomfortable with me having seen him like that.

…

As a side note, I hope you will consider working with a mentor. It's a huge comfort and an enormous confidence builder to be able to pick up the phone to ask a trusted confidant a quick question, a stupid question, or even an embarrassing one. A mentor can save you from making a mistake…or in my case, understand how not to make the same mistake twice.

**Read more about these concepts in the *Aviation Instructor's Handbook*:**

Human factors that inhibit learning

Defense mechanisms

Repression

Denial

Compensation

Projection

Rationalization

Reaction formation

Fantasy

Displacement

# Ricky

Ricky was afraid of stalls. He would perspire just talking about them. When I say he was afraid, I mean that he would cancel any lesson where stalls appeared in the content. Ricky was a certificated flight instructor.

I am afraid of the dentist. It's not a logical fear; there's no reason for me to be afraid. My dentist is a longtime friend. On an intellectual level, I know he would never hurt me and that he has access to all the feel-good drugs for the invasive procedures. Nevertheless, fear is not always a logical thing.

Therefore, when a pilot says that he's afraid of stalls, steep turns, spins or anything else we have to complete during training, I am sympathetic. It may not be a logical fear, but a pilot's fear is very real to him, thus it will affect his performance and the quality of his training experience.

Ricky had completed flight training elsewhere and came to our school for his first flight instructor job. I first became aware of his distaste for stalls during our standardization training, but I didn't realize how bad it was until he started working with clients. Suddenly, it became common knowledge around the school that Ricky didn't like stalls and students should schedule with someone else for those lessons. As chief instructor, this was not acceptable to me.

Ricky's instructor had not been thoughtful in his introduction of stalls. From the way Ricky described his earliest stalls, they were robust.

I knew if Ricky was going to succeed in a flying career, we needed to work through his worst fear. It was time for me to change hats, out of chief mode and into instructor mode.

We started about 4,000 feet AGL in a C172. His hand trembled as he retarded the throttle to about 1,000 RPM. We maintained level flight and allowed the airspeed to bleed-off. When the aircraft started to descend, we kept slowly adding back pressure, as if we wanted to maintain altitude. Soon the stall warning was blaring, but when the stall broke it was not with a big attitude change; it was subtle.

I didn't allow a recovery. Most instructors, when first introducing stalls, are too quick to recover. Directing Ricky's attention to the nose of the aircraft and seeing its relation to the horizon, we spent enough time for him to see the attitude—something he'd not been able to experience before. At the introduction, students need time to perceive the stall.

We maintained the stall. Ricky was encouraged to deflect the ailerons to see how sluggish and unresponsive they were. He experienced the use of rudder pressure to keep the nose straight. Convincing Ricky that he could still control the plane while it was in the stalled condition built his confidence.

By placing the nose slightly below the horizon, Ricky was able to feel the airplane immediately begin to fly again. He experienced how the ailerons were immediately responsive. We repeated this a few times: nose slightly up—stall; nose down—recover. In this way, he could see that the recovery from the stall had nothing to do with power—it was all in the attitude. He enjoyed several recoveries and soaked in the feel of the aircraft. Soon, he was able to detect the subtle feel of the approaching stall, even before the stall warning horn began to buzz.

Fear kept Ricky focused on previous, scary stalls or worried about the future and how the next one might react. I worked to keep him in the present. Slowing down his stall experience helped him to realize that *right now*, he was okay. He was in control. Still in the stall, I pointed at the beautiful sky and reminded him how lucky we were to be smack in the middle of it. However, the vertical speed indicator painted a high rate of descent.

To recover from the descent, we added power. Power was not part of the stall recovery; it was a recovery from the descent.

This demonstration lasted about three minutes. We lost about 2,000 feet, but it gave Ricky the time needed to see the physics at work. By breaking the stall into baby steps, he felt safe and secure in trusting that the aerodynamics were consistent and would work for him.

For Ricky, it was a gentler, kinder way to learn about stalls, but it was also more realistic. In flight, stalls don't naturally occur with the high attitude that most instructors use in teaching stalls. Hanging the airplane by the prop does nothing to teach a student how to perceive an unintentional stall.

After climbing back to altitude, we repeated the experience, but this time, he extended full flaps for a better view over the nose. With the plane held in the stall condition, he focused on a landmark and used rudder to maintain the nose pointed there. The focal point kept his attention outside. He concentrated on keeping the nose on the land-mark and was soon able to move the rudder only to the extent necessary to offset any rolling by the wing. I saw him beginning to relax.

The last stall for Ricky was the base-to-final turn. Still at altitude, Ricky configured for landing, retarded the throttle, began a 500 fpm descent, and slowly increased the angle of attack. We then rolled into a turn (from base to final) except he slowly applied too much rudder pressure to push the nose through the turn. He had no problem seeing and feeling the oncoming spin.

That was enough for Day 1.

We flew together on Day 2 for more stalls. He demonstrated the business-like attitude that one would expect from a professional flight instructor. The next step was for me, acting as a student pilot, to per-form less than perfect. He walked me through each of the common stall scenarios. I watched closely for any signs of his flinching or discomfort but none was evident. *Good.* I'm not saying that he liked doing stalls, only that he learned to trust the physics involved.

Learning to *teach* stalls is very different from learning to demon-strate stalls. The maneuver above that I taught Ricky was the Falling Leaf. Naval pilots learned it in the 1960s, but you won't find it in many textbooks today. By approaching his problem in baby steps, Ricky was able to conquer each small item, one at a time. We didn't try to use logic to overcome his fear.

...

Many accidents result from a pilot's loss of control of their aircraft. In my opinion, this is due to an overemphasis on modern technology at the expense of basic stick-and-rudder skills. Take the time to allow students to experience the aerodynamics that comes with each maneuver. Break maneuvers down into baby steps so students can see what's required at each step to control the airplane. Step outside of the PTS/ACS-required maneuvers and include the types of maneuvers that require pilots to use many of their senses: sight, feel, hearing. This makes them stronger as a pilot. Look to military and upset training syllabi for ideas.

**Read more about these concepts in the *Aviation Instructor's Handbook:***

Maslow's Hierarchy of Needs: Safety and security

Student emotional reactions

# Emma

Emma giggled throughout the entire preflight inspection. She giggled while stowing her flight bag. She giggled through the engine start and run-up checklists. I had a big grin on my face—the kind that you get when you see someone enjoying themselves. It never occurred to me to ask what was so funny or how a student pilot could be this relaxed during her first Progress Check.

A Progress Check—affectionately known by students and instructors as a Prog Check—is a flight with a senior instructor. Its purpose is to give the student feedback and verify progress up to a point. It's a milestone. As chief instructor, I planned a milestone of some sort (Prog Check, block quiz, etc.) after every five or six lessons. They also provide time to check in with a student to see what they might need from us. Installing these landmarks greatly enhanced our student retention and completion rate. I conducted most of the Prog Checks at the flight school.

At Prog Check 1, Emma would have about five hours of flight. This Prog Check was a verification of her abilities in preflight activities and included items like the preflight inspection, cockpit management, checklists, engine start, run-up, radio communication, ground maneuvering, and basic attitudes, followed by post-flight procedures.

Emma was a successful, professional woman of about 55. She was a favorite customer around the flight school. She was always in an upbeat mood and always smiling. She was easily amused, even at herself, but she didn't laugh—she giggled. She had a giggle that was infectious to anyone within earshot. It was one of those open, unreserved giggles like you'd hear from a happy two-year-old. When she giggled, I guarantee you could not hold back.

I had not flown with Emma before but I'd seen her around and I knew who she was. The staff was looking forward to hearing what we'd sound like when we finally got together for a flight. Unfortunately, she cancelled our appointment several times. Her primary instructor informed me that she was frightened to fly with the chief, but the instructor didn't know why.

I called Emma. We talked for the most part of an hour, about nothing in particular, just getting to know each other. My strategy, I convinced myself, was nothing less than superb because the following day she managed to show up for our appointment instead of cancelling.

Face to face, it was obvious just how nervous she was. All students were a little apprehensive so I knew how to ease her fears. I started chatting her up and when I got her to giggle, I assumed she was becoming more comfortable. My technique, I persuaded myself, was nothing less than brilliant.

During the preflight inspection, I kept things light but allowed her to tell me what she was checking and why. She giggled. I thought, "This is fun!" My method, I told myself, was nothing less than skillful.

She completed tasks carefully and soon we were in the air. I had concluded the in-flight assessment and we were returning to the airport. She was set up to enter a mid-field, downwind. Her giggles became more distorted. The closer we got to the runway the more forced, painful and louder they became. I recall saying something like "Ok, let's settle down," but she couldn't. She was giggling out of control. I turned my head to look at her. Her cheeks were wet; she'd been crying! Her eyes pleaded, "Help me!" I didn't expect a six-hour pilot to giggle, and cry, *and* fly all at the same time, so I said, "My airplane, I have the controls. ...You Ok?"

"No, but I will be," was the only part of her message that I could comprehend.

After landing, she was not interested in sterile cockpit procedures during the taxi back. No longer giggling, she needed to talk. The speed at which she was spewing words let me know this had been weighing heavily on her. "I will taxi," I said, deciding to let her vent.

She told me that when she got nervous, she giggled—and always had. She was concerned because she could not control it. She knew it was not appropriate in the airplane so her giggle only added to her overall anxiety. She didn't know what to do. She loved flying and was frightened that I would make her quit because of her giggles. With her venting complete, she seemed relieved after it was all out.

Now I could see: this is why she had cancelled me. Getting her to giggle was no brilliant technique, strategy or skill on my part. This poor woman was in real emotional pain and I felt badly now because I had giggled with her. I was kicking myself in the butt for not having recognized it as a problem.

Emma's lesson ended normally. As soon as she'd left, I called a staff powwow. We often found it helpful to talk about students, in an attempt to help each other and help our clients. New instructors and experienced ones would come at problems from different perspectives. Just having a new set of eyes on an issue was often helpful. The staff worked well together as a team and now we came together for Emma. Her primary instructor admitted that he had not recognized her giggles as a symptom of a problem. He was surprised—but then, Emma had not told him anything.

We were brainstorming ideas and listing them on the white board. Soon we had the basis for *Operation Giggles Gone*. The outline was this:

- The primary instructor and I would speak with Emma together so that she'd know we were a team and working for her. We weren't terminating her training—we were supporting her.

- As much as we loved hearing her giggle, we now understood that it caused her pain, so we no longer encouraged it, or giggled at her giggling. Instead, we recognized it as anxiety and worked to help her feel safe.

- We hoped that we wouldn't have to change our curriculum for her training, but it was an option. However, we weren't going to lower our expectations for her performance.

- We slowed the pace of training to introduce fewer new aspects in each lesson and to allow her more time to become comfortable with each new item. We checked in with her often to see it there was anything else she thought we could be doing to help her.

- We encouraged Emma to ride in the backseat with other students to give her additional perspective and help her relax.

Our school offered testing so when the time came for Emma's FAA knowledge exam, the primary instructor solicited the assistance of the proctor. This assured that Emma would have the testing room all to herself. If the need to giggle arose, she would not interfere with anyone else's testing.

Before Emma's practical exam, we assured that she had an opportunity to meet and have Q&A time with the examiner so that she'd be more relaxed. I cornered the examiner and explained, "Emma has a tendency to giggle when she gets nervous. It would help if you didn't join in the giggling or she may not stop." He was a gem. It all worked out. She passed, and as one of his favorite checkrides.

...

Students aren't always forthcoming with all the information that an instructor might like to have. If the instructor does not know there is hidden information to be uncovered, it can make for a challenging training environment. We sometimes have to read between the lines. People with anxiety react in unconventional ways. Laughing or giggling at inappropriate times is one of those universal, classic anxiety responses.

As instructors, we can't cure a student's anxiety. We can only make sure they feel safe and secure. We can let them know that we are on their side. We can be patient and we can set a pace of training that makes them feel at ease. Emma required this emotional support. It played a large role in her flight training success.

As a side note, I hope while reading this story that you were able to see the value of having a different instructor fly occasionally with a student. Whether it's on a syllabus-required Prog Check or something less formal, having a different set of eyes on a student can bring new facts into view.

**Read more about these concepts in the _Aviation Instructor's Handbook_:**

Human needs

Maslow's Hierarchy of Needs

Student emotional reactions

Anxiety

Normal reactions to stress

# Henry

"I don't want to fly with him again! Do _not_ put him on my schedule anymore. He gives me the heebie-jeebies." The flight instructor framing my office door was the third one this week to complain about Henry.

The instructor was insistent that there was something "off" about Henry. "He asked if I'd ever thought about flying the airplane into the ground! He talked about dying the entire flight and wouldn't it be better to 'go' in a plane." The instructor shuddered at the mere thought of flying with his least-favorite student pilot.

I wasn't certain what heebie-jeebies were but I was pretty sure they weren't warm and fuzzy. I trusted my well-trained staff. No doubt about it, there was a problem. Henry was on the schedule to fly the next day, so I changed his appointment to fly with me.

Just after reaching cruise altitude, Henry started talking some seriously strange death and dying stuff that I would classify as seriously Abnormal (with a capital "A"). We're not talking about the stupid things that kids sometimes say. He was colorfully graphic in exquisite detail. It made my skin crawl. He wore a half-smile while he spoke. The expression on his face was as if he was daydreaming about visiting an exotic, tropical paradise. It took about two minutes before the floor of the cockpit started moving with heebie-jeebies. They scratched at my ankles.

I was nearly in a panic to get my hands wrapped around the controls, ASAP. "My plane, I have the flight controls." Simultaneously making a 180-degree turn back to the airport, I called ATC to let them know we were coming *directly* home.

When Henry asked what was going on, I lied. I stated that I had a problem and needed to be on the ground. I acted as if I had forgotten to preflight the instructor and Mother Nature called. When ATC inquired with a, "Wassup?" I replied something along the same lines.

Back on the ramp, I informed Henry, "I can't do this today. Button her up," and I dashed into the office, leaving a bewildered Henry alone to secure the plane.

I raced into the bookkeeper's office and demanded that she write a check for any credit balance that might be in Henry's account. I was verifying that our training records were complete when it occurred to me to write a note in his pilot logbook; he had about 90 hours including about six at our flight school, so I knew he wouldn't be throwing that away.

I recorded our flight time. Then, in the endorsement section, I clearly printed, "If any CFI would like to talk, my name is _____. My phone number is _____." I did the same thing in the back of the logbook in the ground training area.

It was a simple note. It didn't provide any details or personal opinions about what I had just witnessed. Yet, it was unique enough that any CFI would understand it to be a safety flag. It was my way of communicating with any future training provider.

My postflight discussion was clear and direct. I asked him how long he'd been curious "like that" and if he felt his curiosity was "normal." He thought it normal for him. I pleaded with him to speak with a professional and informed him that he could no longer fly here until he did. I handed him the credit remaining from his account and bid him farewell.

Before the door shut behind him, I was on the phone to the FAA Flight Standards Office. The inspector was interested in hearing my story, but I wasn't convinced that he considered it a priority. Next, I phoned the school's Aviation Medical Examiner and told him of my concerns. The AME suggested that I call the FAA Medical Certification Branch and speak directly with the head honchos there. I did.

The doctor at the Medical Certification Branch was sympathetic. He also clearly explained that the FAA was interested in following up with Henry but they had to guard against a situation where someone might simply be angry with Henry. They were cautious against complaints that falsely accused someone. The FAA had to avoid any unwarranted action. I understood but I needed to do all that I could.

I wrote follow-up email letters to both FAA offices. After that, I solicited written statements from each of my flight instructors recording their unique observations. Everything went into a file—just in case.

In the meantime, the dispatcher was sure to inform other staff members that Henry was no longer eligible to train with us. We cancelled Henry's school-related online account access and the security codes on all doors were changed. We moved the aircraft keys to a new secure location and airport security was informed. I didn't think it warranted airport security notification, but I thought, "Better safe than sorry." After that, there was nothing more to do.

It was less than a month later when my phone rang, "Yea, um, you wrote a note in Henry's logbook?" The caller seemed tentative about revealing too much.

"Yes I did," I said. "Are you his new instructor?"

"Yup. Did you...um, notice anything...um, strange about him?"

"Well that depends on if you're referring to his talking about suicide."

The caller was immediately relieved. "Yes! What's that all about?" Now he was excited about the opportunity to speak openly about our situation. He began jabbering so quick that my ears could barely listen fast enough. The instructor had flown only once with Henry but reported his own variation of some nasty heebie-jeebies.

I didn't feel qualified to give advice on what the caller should do but I offered what I had done and gave him the name and contact information for both the FAA inspector and the Medical Branch. I suggested that if the instructor decided to terminate Henry's training, he could recount his observations in a letter to the FAA and cc me. I received an email first thing the next morning and added that letter to my file.

Some would say that I was on a mission to get Henry out of the sky. I was. The intensity of emotion that stirred inside me when he started saying those disturbing things made my stomach churn. It was my first and only encounter with someone seriously Abnormal (with a capital "A"), but my gut had no trouble recognizing it and I'll never forget it.

My attempts to keep Henry grounded were unsuccessful. Ultimately, he completed flight training elsewhere. He achieved a commercial certificate with an instrument rating. Some felt that I was silly to turn away this good business. I'm not sorry. I would do it again.

It was about six months after the phone call from the concerned instructor that I received a second call and a similar conversation with a second instructor about Henry. Henry was adding a multi-engine rating. I added another letter to my file.

I had accumulated a total of five letters in my file, including two from instructors outside of my corral. I packaged everything together, thinking that the bulk now told a different story, and by registered snail mail, sent it to both the inspector and the Medical Branch. That had the desired effect. They were on it. Unfortunately, it was too little, too late.

I can't say for sure if the crash was Henry's way of resolving his curiosity. I can say that it happened on a perfect clear-blue day; the NTSB found no mechanical discrepancies on the plane; and the pilot held a current medical with First Class status. I felt relief that no one else had been hurt.

Today, in consideration of the airline pilot who intentionally flew an airplane into the French Alps, I find no regrets about my actions concerning Henry. If the accident wasn't a matter of Henry resolving his curiosity, then at the very least it was a classic controlled flight into terrain (CFIT) incident, most of which are unresolved in their cause.

There is a time to keep student confidences, to protect them from embarrassment and to earn and protect their trust. On the other hand, there is also a time when it's important *not* to keep student secrets—to protect others. Your gut will know. Listen to it.

...

I recommend that instructors choose one Aviation Medical Examiner to work with. Have all your students see your "preferred AME." Your preferred AME will be a resource to call on with any airman medical concerns that need discussing. If the local AME doesn't have the answers, he can introduce you to those who do.

While we were in the plane together, I lied to Henry. You might not think well of me for that. This book includes a lot of talk about instructors having integrity, and you might believe that in this case I didn't show my best side. Maybe not. I'm not here to promote myself as being any better than anyone else or to preach what values you should have. I only want to encourage you to think about what you expect of yourself.

**Read more about these concepts in the** *Aviation Instructor's Handbook:*

Seriously abnormal students

# 2

stories
about
## the learning
## process

The mission of every lesson is to push the student as high up into the levels of learning as possible. The preflight briefing area is where the student enters the rote and understanding levels. Practice, at the start of each flight lesson, pushes the student into the application level. And at the end of the flight, with a new variation of the task, the student is nudged into correlation.

However, the customer's brain will only allow you to push him into higher levels of learning when he is relaxed, feels safe, and is having a good time. He must know exactly what, why, and how this lesson is important. And, he must feel confident that his efforts are progressing him toward the goal.

The learning process is an emotional process. In this chapter, you'll read about students whose emotional processing required handling in a way that was compassionate but that still upheld the standards of safe piloting.

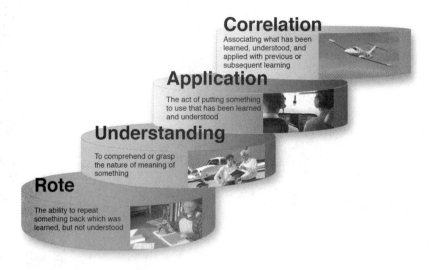

**Figure 2-1.** Learning levels. (FAA)

# Fatima

Fatima's father had sent his teenage daughter to the United States in hopes of providing her with opportunities for a better life. In the short time she had been here, she had assimilated successfully into a Western lifestyle. She learned to speak English. She dressed in jeans and a T-shirt. She wore her hair down and unadorned. With big, round eyes and high cheekbones, she was a classic beauty even without makeup. While attending the university, she worked a part-time job—neither of which women from her native country were known to do. Flight training was a real stretch for her.

She was studious. Fatima could suck up the contents of an FAA handbook quickly, remembering important definitions and concepts. She memorized FARs with ease. She never forgot anything. Regardless of the number of assignments the instructors put on her, she completed them in record time and with near perfection. She scored in the very high 90s on her Private Pilot Knowledge Exam. Bookwork was not her problem.

Neither was motivation. It was obvious that she was a woman with dreams. She didn't want to return to a country where women were not seen as worthy of such aspirations. She appreciated the opportunities allowed her in the United States and she was ready to learn. Unfortunately, none of that translated into her becoming a safe and proficient pilot.

She usually sat quietly in the corner of the classroom by herself. She had a way of sitting that took up the least possible physical space. This was the way in her country. She didn't socialize with other students. She had little to do with anyone. She never laughed—at least not aloud—and seldom smiled. There appeared to be no joy in her heart.

During her first Prog Check, I had difficulty assessing her knowledge. Opening her mouth to speak appeared to be painful, as if she'd recently had extensive dental work. When she did speak, she cast her eyes downward and she used a hushed whisper. I took this as nervousness and decided to go directly to the plane as most students settle down once the engine is spinning.

Around the plane, Fatima moved efficiently. I complimented her on a thorough preflight. She shrugged it off. The cold engine roared to life on her first attempt to start, despite needing extra prime. I gave Fatima a robust, "All right!" Her expression appeared to say, "What are you so excited about?" I began to suspect she wasn't comfortable accepting compliments.

Her submissive nature showed in the way she handled the plane. Her feather light touch on the throttle didn't demand the plane to move. Neither did her light-footed pressure on the brakes command it to stop. I finally said, "Come on: make this hunk of metal do what you want it to do." She couldn't bring herself to trust herself.

A major problem showed itself on the radio. Her meek and mild manner, coupled with her soft-spoken voice and her unclear message drove ATC crazy. She began every radio call with "If it pleases you, may I …" I decided things would move along smoother if I handled the radio and she concentrated on the plane.

During flight, I saw no positive aircraft control. She allowed the plane to fly willy-nilly. I began with constant but gentle encouragement for her to take control—to be in command. Assuming she was still nervous, I tried to keep things light but none of my normal ploys for helping students relax seemed to work. We were airborne for about 30 minutes when, convinced that I was displeased with her, she began to cry. Time to land.

Returning to the debrief area, I asked Fatima what she thought of the flight. Her assessment was entirely negative. When I suggested a few things that I thought she could be pleased with, she was quick to correct me. She overemphasized even the slightest imperfections in her performance. I ended the lesson there, unsure of what to do or say. She had the know-how but not the self-esteem to be pilot-in-command.

If learning starts with perceptions, then Fatima's success *at anything* in life was in jeopardy because of her most basic perception: the way she viewed herself. Her perception was not reality. She discarded the hardworking, intelligent, talent inside her and saw only mistakes and negatives.

The next time I saw Fatima was for her Prog Check retake. I knew the instructors had been working with her on radio communications. I hoped they had also worked on her self-concept and esteem. She and I huddled while I laid out specifically what the objectives were for passing the flight check. She seemed to understand.

It wasn't a great flight but the improvement was enough. Yet, she wasn't willing to accept my assessment of her satisfactory performance. I had to prove to her that she had earned it. I replayed the flight, minute-by-minute, comparing her performance against the objectives we had agreed to. She finally had to accept it.

Prog Check Two also required two attempts to pass—not because she wasn't a capable pilot, but because she didn't *believe* that she was a capable pilot. She wasn't able to let go of her negative self-image. Fatima grew up in an environment where women were second-class citizens. A woman, in her opinion, had no reason to feel proud or capable.

Still, she wasn't a quitter.

I aimed to make her mentally strong. I began using a closed fist, raised in the air, like inner-city gang members would use as a greeting to one another. She was required to return the fist greeting to me. It was a reminder of the strength that I saw inside her even though she could not yet see it.

Prog Check Three required three attempts to pass. At this point, she had accumulated 30 hours and had not yet soloed. We were still playing our game. I would raise my fist in the air with a face of determination. She would show her perfect teeth in a big smile and raise her fist to me. I returned the smile with a nod. Even though I was not passing her on Prog Checks, she knew that I wanted good things for her.

The woman had moxie. I liked that, but with 50 flight hours, Fatima still had not soloed. Sadly, I knew it was time for *the* talk. Like almost all instructors, I hate *the* talk. The one that says that instructors have done all that we can as individuals and as a team. The one that says, "It's just not happening." I hate how I feel like a failure as an instructor when we have to have *the* talk. On the other hand, I do not feel good about continuing to take a student's money once serious doubts are undeniable about the student ever achieving a pilot's certificate. Professional integrity demands that an instructor be honest with a client.

*The* talk must be frank. It must be clear. It must be brutally honest but delivered with compassion. It's done privately. Throughout *the* talk, I am sure to separate the person from their performance. I don't want to damage a personal relationship with the client; I want to minimize the damage to their ego. The goal is to keep their defense mechanisms at bay. I only address the problem. The problem is the topic of conversation. I never say *you* did this or *you* didn't do that. I say things like, "I'm still not seeing a pilot-in-command sitting in the seat next to me" and "I'm still not hearing the authority-voice of an airline captain on the radio."

When the situation absolutely requires me to say *you*, I say instead, *we*. *We* did this.... *We* didn't do that.... In this way, I am not assigning blame to a client. I am taking part ownership and responsibility in the problem and for its solution. Clients can feel a level of support and know that they don't carry the burden alone.

Fatima begged me not to give up on her. She knew it would cost more money than initially expected and she was fine with that. She was willing to do any work assigned to her, so long as she could continue training. She desperately wanted to be a pilot and to remain a part of the school's family.

Even though I was completely certain that she would never graduate, I gave in. If she was intent on doing this and willing to do the work, I would assure her we were there for her. But there had to be conditions. I didn't want her father, or anyone else, to think the school was taking advantage of her, or that any instructor was using her to build his hours.

Throughout the coming weeks, instructors were clear to document real and tangible improvements—no matter how small—so that she could see progress. We celebrated every milestone with photos posted on social media. I hoped that seeing progress and her receiving comments from other students on her accomplishments would be motivational. We also divided the content of her lesson plans in half, so she'd have more time to get comfortable with each maneuver. The praise given to her was genuine and specific so she would feel that she had earned it.

The staff worked to bring her out of her shell, and to talk more about what interested her outside of flying. We made sure she attended several of the safety seminars, pancake breakfasts and other fun aviation activities in the area. She needed to know that we liked her, accepted her, and were supportive of her. We made sure that she met other students who had struggles and who eventually found success. She rode in the backseat with some of our other students who had challenges. We engaged her on a personal level, at every opportunity.

For her part, she acknowledged her low self-image. It wasn't completely her fault, though; it had been the culture from her native country. She had to overcome beliefs ingrained into her from a very young age.

She agreed to work on becoming more extroverted. She agreed that this was the main problem holding her back from success. She agreed to benchmarks and goal dates for accomplishing smaller training goals. She knew there had to be some measurable, incremental progress. She understood that we would not lower our expectations. She had to meet the standard, but she could take the time she needed.

We wrote up an agreement, using bulleted talking points to recap everything and we put it in the file. I was still guarding against any perception of impropriety on behalf of either the instructors or the school.

Fatima, to my surprise, did eventually earn a private pilot certificate. She danced and pranced as I had never seen anyone do. It had taken two years. I have no idea how many hours she had.

I was wrong about Fatima's ability to complete training and achieve a pilot certificate. As a result, I stopped trying to predict which student would or would not be successful. I train with anyone who desires to do the work. You just can't see what perseverance and motivation might be within someone.

Understanding basic psychology is important for an instructor. It helps to separate what may be a problem personality trait of the student versus a flaw in the training style of the instructor. For Fatima, learning to fly was a psychological process, not a logical one.

Read more about these concepts in the *Aviation Instructor's Handbook:*

The learning process—A psychological process, not a logical one

Perceptions

Factors that affect perception

Goals and values

Self-concept

Time and opportunity

Element of threat

...

A flight instructor is not a psychologist; we can't cure every problem a client brings into the cockpit. All we can do as instructors is be their advocates. We worked to give Fatima every tool for success. We gave her extra time and we removed the elements that made her feel threatened.

# Dillon

It was a gray February day. Not a nice one for flying. I sat down with a big mug of hot chocolate topped with a pyramid-shaped mound of whipped cream to begin reading the latest email.

Dear Arlynn,

We've never met. I'm a flight instructor of about two years. I haven't accumulated many hours, being at a small airport. I'm the only flight instructor for miles around and I work alone. I haven't found a support network of instructors to bounce ideas off. I've been pulling my hair out with a problem student and am hoping you might lend some advice.

The student is a retirement age but not elderly. He has 35 hours including 10 consecutive lessons in the traffic pattern, flying twice a week. The problem is twofold:

1. He can't remember procedures or how he's done things before—not just lesson-to-lesson but lap-to-lap in the pattern. Every lap he does different. One lap he remembers procedures, the next he can't. One lap he extends flaps on final; the next it's on crosswind. Quizzing him before the flight doesn't help. Having him study at home doesn't help. Repetition doesn't help.

2. He doesn't recognize when things don't look right. One lap he'll do a lovely go-around; the next he'll retract all the flaps, all at once, add full power and point the plane <u>at the earth</u>. The earth hurling toward us doesn't set off alarms with him. I have to intervene to save us.

Most concerning is that he'll appear to make progress for several lessons and then suddenly relapse in dramatic fashion. The last half-dozen lessons we've done have been good, most completely unassisted. Today you'd think he was on lesson three: couldn't figure out pitch and power; wild and crazy go-arounds; and, when I pointed out that he still had takeoff-flaps extended on crosswind his response was to extend full flaps, which he insisted we have always done. Even if I can get him through a solo, I don't know if I'll ever get him further. Ideas?

Thank you in advance,
Dillon

Dillon, Nice to meet you! If you are asking for my opinion, I believe this to be a classic case of learning plateau. Take this boy on a fun cross-country and he'll be fine! Let me know how it turns out.

Your friend, Arlynn

Arlynn,

I appreciate your willingness to help and I would never disrespect you by disagreeing with someone of your experience, but honestly, don't you think it must be something more? I mean, are you sure that you gave my case careful analysis? I just don't think this is a simple plateau. It's an ocean of misery.

Dillon

Dillon, It's only a "simple plateau" when it happens to someone else. Yep, I'm sure. I'll bet a tall mug of hot chocolate on it! Let me know how the cross-country goes! Have fun.

Arlynn

I'm sorry but I can't see wasting this poor man's money on a cross-country given his training success to date.

It's his money. Let him decide: Do something really cool and completely new, or run circuits around the traffic pattern... again. Let me know what he says!

OK readers, let's you and I break this down.

*Ten consecutive lessons in the traffic pattern.* Really? That's enough to turn any gifted student into a bored, incapable, brain-dead zombie. Students need plenty of landing practice, but it's up to the instructor to keep it fresh, interesting and stimulating. Why not include a few landings at the end of each "regular" maneuver lesson? How about planning a scenario; practice maneuvers en route to a second, local airport; and practice landings there before maneuvering back home. As another option, bump him up into the cross-country phase and include extra landings at each destination airport.

*The last half dozen lessons have been good, with most completely unassisted.* It doesn't get any better than a student who can perform a half-dozen lessons without assistance! Why are we still here, doing the same thing? Move on. If the student has previously been troublesome, I might not solo him after a single unassisted lesson but I'd think of something challenging—something different—to build his confidence, and mine, that he was indeed ready to solo.

I wouldn't even tackle his apparent symptoms until we fix the problem: the learning plateau. Everything else mentioned is a symptom of the problem. I was certain of it.

Every month for more than a decade, I ran a classroom-style initial flight instructor ground school. Each month we did an exercise to illustrate the learning plateau. Year in and year out, the results were remarkably consistent. Participants had a leveling-off of learning after the third attempt, followed by a downward trend. Then for the next four or five additional attempts, there was some very slight improvement only to be followed by another, dramatic downward trend. Twelve months of ground school, for ten years, with an average of five participants—that's 600 learning plateau graphs! Who can argue with such scientific data and analysis?

Not only did the exercise illustrate the learning plateau, it also proved to me that an instructor could—unknowingly—induce a learning plateau, by *over practicing* a skill. It's like a rash: scratching it doesn't improve it. I maintained a strict training standard operating procedure (SOP) never to repeat any lesson more than three times. Period. To do so would only cost the student money and cause frustration for me. If at the end of the third attempt, the student still didn't "get it," then the student would fly with another, alternate instructor.

Many times an alternate instructor will witness immediate and positive results with the student, and he doesn't have to do a thing. The alternate instructor doesn't have to be a better instructor than I, just different. Having any new stimulus in the training environment, even a different instructor in the cockpit, will normally fix the problem. However, if the student has a real problem, an alternate instructor can provide a different viewpoint, all to the benefit of the student. The more different perspectives a student can get on a problem, the faster and better his insights will come.

If you are like Dillon and don't have an alternate instructor, then get creative. Mix it up. Do something that makes the lesson different. Go to a new portion of the syllabus that does not require the problem skill. Don't continue to do the same thing over and over and expect different results.

Many times the primary instructor is reluctant to allow "their student" to fly with an alternate for fear that the student will prefer to continue training with the alternate. The primary instructor is fearful of losing a client. My response is, "Get over yourself." Our job is to help students learn. Sometimes, that might mean getting out of their way.

An instructor's only concern should be the well-being and possible benefits to the student. It's not about you. Focus on what's best for the student above all else. A student will always prefer an instructor who has his best interest in mind.

A learning plateau can be equally frustrating for the instructor. As you can see from Dillon's letter, he was "pulling his hair out." Then, once the student begins to sense the instructor is frustrated, the student's performance will wane, making it that much worse.

I don't know of any instructor who is excited about 10 consecutive lessons in the traffic pattern. The fastest way to suck the joy out of a new instructor is to wind him up into a bored, brain-dead zombie circling the traffic pattern. Fresh and stimulating lessons are better for everyone involved.

Learning plateaus are real and they can be devastating to a student and frustrating for the instructor. Rather than trying to identify and fix a plateau, a better plan is not to allow one to develop.

...

Dillon is a very good instructor; I don't mean for this story to put him in poor light. First, he cared about his student. Second, he reached out for advice. I'm not sure why, but that is uncommon with flight instructors—especially newly certificated ones. Perhaps a new instructor mistakenly believes that he *should* know everything. It's hard on an ego to admit you don't know everything, but even doctors get second opinions, as do lawyers and many other professions. Getting a second opinion marks you as a professional.

Dillon reported that a couple of cross-countries did make the student happy and relaxed. He was able to solo his problem student soon after.

**Read more about these concepts in the** *Aviation Instructor's Handbook:*

Learning plateaus

Types of practice

# Edsel

"He called me a son-of-a-bitch!" I was excited, jumping for joy. My mentor gave me a congratulatory high-five. Other people nearby were curious as to why I was so pleased to be called a SOB.

Edsel was almost ancient. He had been a World War II ace naval pilot. He still wore his hair in a strict military buzz but his thin face was usually two or three days unshaven. He always wore a Fedora, even in the summer, which he gently removed and carefully placed in the backseat of the airplane. He was the consummate gentleman and found it uncomfortable to board the Beechcraft Debonair before me. As pilot, he boarded first, unable to hold the single, right-side door for me as I boarded or help me in, as a chivalrous man would.

He'd flown a lifetime before I was born. He'd been in combat missions to places I couldn't pronounce and even landed on aircraft carriers. In his youth, he had won dogfights over faraway islands throughout the South Pacific. He had unbelievable, sit-on-the-edge-of-your-seat stories about struggling to keep limp and broken airplanes flying back to his home base. Yet, with all that experience, he was not instrument-rated.

He had called Charlie inquiring about instrument instruction but Charlie had a boatload of students and recommended that Edsel fly with me. He was not keen about accepting me as a possible replacement. With children much older than I, he seemed to view me as a child. In his mind, he needed a rough and tough instructor who would yell and shout him into being a precise instrument pilot. How could he possibly learn important lessons from someone the age of his grandchildren?

"No," Edsel said, "I am used to the military way. I need a commanding presence to push me hard." Charlie was persistent, "Look, fly with her for 5 hours. If you don't like her then I promise to find room for you on my schedule." He made the deal.

I was still a new flight instructor. "What do I do to earn his respect?" I wanted to know how I should teach to meet Edsel's needs. "Just be you," was Charlie's only advice.

Any instructor would have worked well with Edsel. He was amenable. He politely asked intelligent and practical questions, although they often required hours for me to research to find answers. He wasn't satisfied with only knowing the *what*. He wasn't content until I could tell him *why* and *how* things worked. That was just the way his brain worked, strictly in the cognitive domain. I became a regular visitor to the maintenance department, soliciting assistance from the technicians. Edsel insisted on knowing why that thingamajig was there and how it connected to that whatchamacallit. I learned a lot about airplane systems because of spending time with Edsel. He was giving me a fair chance and I worked hard to answer each of his questions.

Nonetheless, in the cockpit he still cared for me as he would a youngster, inquiring about the temperature (Was I comfortable?) and regarding my seat adjustment (Was I relaxed?). Like a grandfather, he was on alert for any small thing I needed and how he might attend to me.

Before a student can accept the instructor's assessment, they must first accept the instructor. What they don't say in the textbooks is *how* to earn the trust and respect of a student, especially when the student is much older or more experienced.

Edsel liked to negotiate my lesson objectives. I would often show him the objective for the lesson but then Edsel would elevate it. He wanted to accomplish more and push himself. After meeting my objective, he knew we could return home but he never returned with pride unless he pushed himself to the limit. I learned that if I could make him want it he would push hard to accomplish it. I used that.

We were practicing the Vertical-S, a proficiency-building maneuver that starts out as easy but becomes increasingly difficult as it progresses. Near the end, the pilot is required to focus completely. Edsel was doing as well as one would expect but grew bored with the monotony of the maneuver. I threatened, in a playful way, that he should enjoy this because the next lesson would be much more difficult. Five minutes later, he begged to try the next maneuver. I thought that might happen.

Scheduled for the next lesson was the Vertical $S_1$—the same maneuver but with the addition of 90-degree heading changes, left then right. It greatly pumped up the difficulty level. As I expected, Edsel was anxious to fly the $S_1$ that day. He was doing pretty well but was struggling and concentrating intently. I intended to make one small suggestion that would help. Only two words had escaped my mouth when he suddenly launched an onslaught of colorful sailor-type curse words I'd never heard before. The grand finale was when he blurted out in complete frustration and anger, "You son of a bitch!" He suddenly caught himself. Embarrassed, he apologized and resumed his silent focus on the maneuver.

It happened so fast I almost missed it. He had just given me the highest compliment. I was happy with the label of SOB because it said, at that moment, Edsel stopped viewing me as a little girl. At that moment, he accepted me as an instructor. I had motivated him to push himself and in learning how to motivate him, I had grown into the kind of instructor he needed. I made it. Charlie would not be reshuffling his schedule to make room for Edsel.

Edsel was an overachiever. He worked hard and he expected his instructor to work hard. I had to prepare for the lesson *and* the next lesson because he often progressed faster than I expected. I sensed that if he became disappointed once, my credibility was shot.

The overachieving student will have questions—lots of them. If you don't know the answer, tell them that. Then do your research and follow-up with them later. Don't try to B.S. them with a half-answer. Edsel could sniff out B.S. from a mile away and would shut me down immediately saying, "Get me answers when you can." I could tell that he knew when I didn't know something with the depth that he thought I should.

The overachieving student will require you to study the POH. Up to this point, you've probably had someone to help you learn an unfamiliar airplane. Now, as an instructor, you will most likely teach yourself an unfamiliar airplane so you can then teach it to the student. I had not flown Edsel's type of plane before and had to learn which power settings and configurations would work best for precision instrument work.

If there is a maintenance shop on your airport, count yourself lucky! The professionals in maintenance are your best friend during the first years as an instructor—at least they should be. I suggest you get to know them before you need them. They can teach you everything you need to know about a specific airplane. I promise you will not become an expert on a plane without a helpful tech.

Pilot manuals only take you so far. They are great for operating the plane—for showing which switch needs flipping to do so-and-so—but to understand the systems and how the systems work together, pilot manuals are lacking. Your maintenance tech has access to repair manuals with drawings and explanations. A good tech can explain a system to you in a heartbeat and make it sound like poetry.

Edsel and I continued to work together. He received his instrument rating in short order. I graduated a good instrument pilot but the truth is he made me a much better instructor.

**Read more about these concepts in the** *Aviation Instructor's Handbook:*

Characteristics of learning

Learning styles

Motivation

Presenting new challenges

# 3

## stories
### about

## effective
## communication

The sigh…. It's not a word but it speaks volumes. It doesn't have the same meaning for everyone. When a man let's out a loud sigh, it usually means he's content. I can say, being female—and you married men can back me up on this—that when a woman exhales a loud sigh it usually means she thinks you are an idiot. If she puts her hand on her hip and sighs, she's completely fed up; and, oh my gosh, if she puts her hand on her hip and pushes her hip out to one side and sighs, then you better get out of there—your life may be in danger. I won't go into the eye roll, the crossed arms or the foot tap. Those are beyond the scope of this book.

Communication is about getting your message across to the other person. My best advice on doing this effectively is to use the same rules that your mother taught you: Be pleasant. Smile. Sit up straight. Look people in the eye when you speak. Open your mouth and annunciate properly. Use your manners with please and thank you. Don't use foul language, don't talk about things you don't know about and don't gossip. If it's not true, kind, or necessary, then don't speak it. Take responsibility for your side, whether as sender or receiver, to get the job done as painlessly as possible.

In this chapter, you'll read about circumstances where communication was, shall we say…interesting.

**Figure 3-1.** Instructor communication tools. (FAA)

# Pilot-People

Through my stories, you have come to know my students and customers. Now, my question is: If you were to write a book about your students, how well could you describe them? Do you have enough detail to create them as a character in a story? Do you know what's important to them and what motivates them? What frightens them, and how do you console them? These kinds of personal details allow us to form relationships that make us effective instructors.

The role of the instructor as an effective communicator is everything. Regardless of student background, gender, or curriculum, being able to relate to people is your starting point. You have to start with who the student is—what they care about and what they already know—and then you teach around that. The underlying message in the effective instructor's communication is always, "I believe you can do this and I'll help you."

My teaching style includes a presentation of the book material, and then my commentary on the material. The commentary is my experience and value-added not found in the text. It's a little piece of me that I gift to them. It's based on what I think is important. It's how I interject the personal habits and thought processes I want to instill in clients. The book material gets them through the test; the commentary teaches that *other* important information.

The commentary is a discussion. I draw them out. We compare thought processes and priorities. If I know how a student thinks then I never worry about what he'll do. If I don't know how he thinks, then I'm scared to let him out of my sight.

If you are alert and aware while teaching, you know there are certain areas where students will have trouble. An effective communicator designs instructional techniques to handle difficult areas, in advance. Collect a few metaphors and analogies that you can offer at the drop of a hat.

A pleasant way to start getting to know anyone is with an open question: "Tell me about you." In the next lesson, I'd ask something like, "What do you like to do when not flying?" If I want to know how to motivate them, I ask, "Why do you think you've been so successful at (fill in the blank)." It's both a compliment as well as revealing. What drove the person to be successful in one aspect of their life will probably lead them to success as a pilot.

As they begin to share details about themselves, I share similar ones. I want them to know enough about me to become comfortable. That way, when they need to share a fear or concern, they feel at ease. When I find areas of common interest, I dive right in to expand on it. This too requires practice. Choose what of yourself you are comfortable revealing. Your students will be loyal to you because they like you as a person and trust you. Be human with them.

Pay attention to how you are communicating. Pay attention to the tone of your voice and your body language. If you are excited and passionate with one aspect but not so much with another, students will notice your passion and assume that's the more important point. Pay attention to your timing. Why did you spend twenty minutes on this topic and only five minutes on that? While some topics take longer to explain, students will usually suppose the longer time spent was due to importance.

You might look at the stories in this book and think I had weird students. No, they weren't weird (…well, maybe one or two were). The fact is that the world is full of weird people. As the saying goes, "Everyone is weird except you and me and sometimes I wonder about you." Students are individuals. Help them deal with the issues that arise in the plane, but also with the issues that arise outside of the plane when it affects the way they make decisions.

# Susan

Susan panicked. It occurred often and was to me, her instructor, a rather bothersome habit. Not just that, but she would scream, "Oh my!" and simultaneously throw both hands up in a surrender position and twist her head to the side. She didn't wish to see what she assumed to be an impending crash. When my headset filled with the rush of her deep inhale, I knew it would be immediately followed by, "Oh my." This was my cue to reach for the yoke; she was about to abandon all aircraft control.

Susan worked as a receptionist at the front desk of the fixed base operator. She had a reputation of being an airhead. It was well earned; but then, she was an average spunky teenager. I assumed she was just excited about life in general. She was very enthusiastic about becoming an aviatrix.

She was an excellent student, intelligent, disciplined, and ambitious. She was on time for appointments with each assignment completed. She flew with precision and was never satisfied to be merely plus-or-minus 100 feet. Despite being a flighty female, she came to the airplane with a business-like attitude. In the air, she was careful and diligent. Unfortunately, I could not predict her cockpit panic attacks. When flying with Susan, I had to sit tall in the seat, poised for action. Close student supervision required me to remain on high alert.

Anything unexpected would send Susan into this panic mode. A stall that broke abruptly, a slight gust of wind on final, or a bounced landing were all precursors to one of her bouts. We talked about it. I encouraged her to ride backseat on other student's flights so she could preview upcoming lessons. I made every effort to lessen any unexpected events with a thorough preflight discussion and by instructing clearly in the cockpit. I don't like surprises either.

As a result of Susan, I developed a favorite phrase: "instructional surprise." It's when a student does exactly what I tell them to do. Unfortunately, they do exactly what I say rather than what I mean.

For instance, if I yelled *"POWER!!"* Susan didn't realize that I expected her to *add* power or that I wanted *a lot* of it, *right now.* Her performance improved when I said things like, "full power NOW!" She did equally as well with, "add just enough power to hear the RPM change." I didn't tell her to add 200 RPM, especially if on low final, because I didn't want to divert her attention inside the cockpit to look at the tach. She even responded correctly to phrases like, "add *just* a smidgeon of power." The emphasis on *just* always yielded the desired result.

I could also suggest power adjustments by describing the position of the throttle. Phrases like "throttle to idle" or "full throttle" were helpful to her.

My first instructional surprise came while teaching Susan to start the engine. We were discussing each checklist item and she was doing a fabulous job. "Feet on the brakes" was not on the checklist. I was surprised when immediately after the engine roared to life, the airplane tried to skid across the ramp at near takeoff speed. Luckily, I regained my senses, retarded the throttle and stomped on the brakes. She had done exactly what I had told her to do—only that and nothing more. That instructional surprise was my fault.

She was very concerned about stalls. They made her nervous. On an early stall lesson, I demonstrated one and its recovery before exchanging controls with her. Her stall didn't break cleanly. We were descending without her realizing that we were no longer flying. I calmly instructed, "Nose down, recover from the stall." I thought that was clear enough.

Susan, being the good student that she was, did exactly that. She straight-armed the controls, sending the airplane almost vertical, the spinner pointed at the ground. Every pencil that every student had ever dropped in the cockpit rose to my chin level and hovered in the zero-gravity environment. Dust, dirt and debris became airborne. It took just a second for me to recover from my surprise and our unusual attitude. This one was my mistake. After that, I learned to say *how much* to put the nose down. Telling her "nose down, to *just* below the horizon" or "nose down a *wee* bit" advanced Susan's performance greatly, especially with some emphasis on *wee.*

There was a similar problem on one of Susan's early takeoffs when I probably said something like "nose up." Yep, you guessed it. The stall warning had just begun to sing when I recovered us to a normal climb attitude. From then on, I always instructed exactly where to put the nose rather than giving an unspecific request.

I recommend you avoid instructional surprises whenever possible. When you hear an instructor talk about students trying to kill them, it's more likely that the instructor had not yet learned what Susan taught me: that students need to know what to do and *how much* to do it. We've all heard the problems that occur when we ass/u/me!

···

Let's talk more about student supervision but in a slightly different vein.

While most instructors are well versed in FARs, they are not familiar with the requirements of the aircraft insurance policy. For solo flights by a student pilot, nearly every aircraft policy has a "Direct Supervision Clause" (or something closely resembling that title). It will require a student pilot to receive the approval of and be under the direct supervision of an instructor for every flight, from engine start to engine shutdown.

While the specific definition of direct supervision is in that particular insurance policy, they all carry similar logic. Therefore, a good training SOP, one that will ensure that every solo for a student pilot meets the insurance requirements, would have the instructor at the airport immediately prior to the student pilot's departure to evaluate the conditions and give an approval for solo. A few examples of items to assess include:

- *The airport*—possible taxiway maintenance, runway closures, inoperative NAVAIDs, NOTAMs, TFRs, or airspace issues (such as nearby parachute operations)

- *The aircraft*—maintenance discrepancies, status of inspections, and a proper preflight inspection

- *The flight*—fuel reserves, possible alternatives, and plans for the student to return before dark

- *The weather*—ceilings, visibility, wind, and possible forecasts for rapidly changing conditions

- *The student*—observe if he is mentally engaged, rested and excited about the flight; verification of endorsements

At our school, each student was dispatched with their lesson plan. It indicated where the student was to fly, maneuvers to practice, required time of return, and the instructor's initials to show that the lesson objectives were reviewed with the student prior to launch. This was the instructor's specific approval for the student pilot's flight. It also ensured the student knew where to fly, what to practice, and when to be home. After the flight, it was filed in the training folder.

It's worth spending a few minutes to review the aircraft insurance policy. Making sure that the insurance will cover a loss is an important reason to provide direct supervision. In my opinion, however, the primary reason to provide direct student supervision is to enhance safety by assuring that you are on hand to launch a safe and enjoyable flight for the student.

**Read more about these concepts in the *Aviation Instructor's Handbook:***

Basic elements of communication

Barriers to effective communication

Developing communication skills

Lack of common experience

# Abe

"I have a client for you," the boss told me after sliding into the overstuffed chair behind his desk. "He's retiring from Delta Airlines and just purchased a C172. He needs to get current in a single-engine. He wants an instructor who won't be intimidated and I figure you're the least intimidate-able instructor here. He's yours if you want him!" As a relatively new instructor, I was excited to get up close to a real-life airline pilot and get first-hand tips on one day flying the heavy metal.

I found a few minutes to contemplate a training strategy before my new client arrived. I wanted to be prepared. I assumed he would require three takeoffs and landings and perhaps a flight review to meet aeronautical recency requirements. Additionally, he might need an extra hour in the C172 for proficiency. At most, I thought he would need maybe two hours of flight plus an hour on the ground for the flight review. *Piece of cake.*

Even without his uniform, Abe was the quintessential airline captain. At 60-something, he was wide in the shoulders and slender in the hips. He had a neatly manicured, full cover of salt and pepper hair. In addition to a pleasant face, he possessed "command presence"—the kind you only learn from being in the military.

Our first appointment was said to be a planning meeting but I knew it was an interview before he agreed to allow me to be his instructor. He was old; I was young…and a female. I got it. We scheduled an hour to plan his training but I'd already made the plan. I only needed to sell him on it. I expected to be eating a Big Mac in 10 minutes.

Abe said a lot with few words. There was no fluff, just the facts. I liked that. We communicated effectively. I learned that he had already hired and fired another instructor because he felt that instructor was not doing the job. *Uh-oh, better be on my toes.*

Abe's latest gig was flying the L-1011 trans-Atlantic routes. *How cool!* As he sat, recapping a lively multi-decade flying career, it was starting to dawn on me that my initial assessment and training plan were woefully lacking in important areas. He went on for several more minutes. When he was finally finished, I felt the need to recap from the notes I had been franticly scribbling, "Let me ask a few questions just to make sure I understand what you are telling me." I needed to check that my perceptions were correct—that I hadn't misunderstood. "If I have this right, then...you don't normally conduct the airplane preflight inspection?"

"Oh no," he chuckled, "Not in the last 25 years or so. That's a first officer's job."

"...and you don't normally check weather, calculate weight-and-balance or make flight preparations?"

"No. Those are dispatcher duties."

"Do you fly VFR?"

"Nope."

"Are you knowledgeable in general-aviation regulations?"

"Probably not. In the military we had the military way and for the past 25 years I've followed airline procedures and ops specs which are somewhat different than FARs."

"...anything else?" I hoped he would offer more if I left the question open-ended.

"Yea, I'm sure there's much more but I don't know what I don't know. Your world is foreign to me. We don't share common experiences even though we're both in aviation. That's why I'm here, to learn. I want to keep flying. I just need help with the transition into general aviation. You seem to get it. Will you help me?" Soon, 10 minutes had turned into 60. I got the job but not the Big Mac.

Abe was enthusiastic to be in the plane. "You handle the radio, kid, and I'll take care of the metal." He always called me "kid" but said it with affection and a twinkle in his eye. I never minded. That day he learned about single-pilot resource management.

Over the weeks that followed, we discovered the many differences between flying at 30,000 feet and 3,000—mainly, the visibility is "zilch down here." The first time a bug went splat on the windshield, Abe just about jumped out of his seat. He insisted we must have had a mid-air collision.

Throughout his training, I found myself tweaking my original lesson plan. His knowledge of general-aviation protocols had holes, like Swiss cheese, that needed filling. Abe complained about the lack of "valet parking" so I introduced him to a motorized hand-tug. He missed his "cockpit coffee" so I introduced him to the Thermos. However, when I introduced him to the "Little John," it was abstract; the concept had no meaning to him. He roared a belly-busting laugh, wiping away tears with a white cotton handkerchief. Then he saw that I was serious about its purpose.

Hunched over a VFR sectional chart, we debated suitable visual checkpoints. When I said "checkpoints," Abe thought the Pacific, the Atlantic and possibly the Mississippi were all that were required. We were saying the same word, but conjuring up very different images!

Abe was an exemplary "student" and I knew that our time together would soon be complete. He had just grabbed the engine shutdown checklist when I said, "Hold on, a second…don't shutdown." He looked quizzical. I explained, "I'd like you to solo."

Abe cocked his head a little to one side in disbelief and confusion. "You WHAT?" Lowering his chin, he gazed over the top of his wire-rimmed reading glasses with a look that burned clear through. "Kid, are you really going to treat me like a student pilot? I have learned a few things from you, but you DO realize that I have a boatload of hours, right?" He appeared insulted, getting emotional rather than listening.

"Hold on a sec," I said, trying to make him understand why I thought it important. "When was the last time you flew an airplane solo—by yourself?" His face contorted through a series of emotions as he clicked backward through the years to realize that he couldn't remember *ever* flying alone in the cockpit.

"That's right," he reflected, "I learned to fly during World War II in transport planes and then went to work for Delta immediately after."

Without warning, he slapped his thigh and boomed, "Ok! Let's do this." Suddenly he was animated and nervous like any student pilot on first solo. Afterward, he made me take several photos and cut the back from his expensive shirt. He wanted the complete solo experience.

When first assessing my new client, I made the usual new-instructor mistake of making assumptions about a student without first getting to know him, listening to his story and asking questions. I made rigid lesson plans that included strict objectives. It took a while to learn that I needed to be flexible and to allow time for those unplanned teaching opportunities that popped up unexpectedly. Sometimes, those unanticipated teachable moments were the most effective.

As I understood it, the fired instructor—the one who came before me—had made the mistake of feeling inept sitting next to a pilot of seemingly more experience. It's a common problem: when a new instructor works with a very experienced pilot, the instructor begins to doubt his value. The new instructor thinks, "I can't possibly teach this guy anything," and so, he cannot.

...

What many new instructors fail to realize is how vast and diverse aviation is, from the smallest light sport airplane to the fastest military jet to the largest jumbo airliner; from banner towing to air taxi to aerial firefighting; from the most modern G2000 cockpit to one with a basic six-pack. A pilot might have a lot of experience in one corner of aviation. However, when it's time to change corners, the transition is easier and safer with an instructor having experience in that specific area. Even a newly certificated instructor has much to offer an experienced pilot seeking help.

**Read more about these concepts in the *Aviation Instructor's Handbook*:**

Lack of common experience

Confusion between the symbol and the symbolized object

Abstractions

Listening

Questioning

Open-ended questions

Getting emotional rather than listening

Making assumptions

# Carlos

I attended high school with one of Carlos's six sons. I enjoyed my charming classmate so I was intrigued to meet the father. Carlos and his wife had immigrated to the United States from Central America during their college years. He had built a successful, private oncology practice. He spoke softly with a heavy Mexican accent and he started every sentence with my name. He made it sound musical, like the way Ricardo Montalban would say it.

One of the many benefits of being a flight instructor is that students will always take your call. No matter how busy they are, when their flight instructor calls you are never screened and seldom placed on hold.

Still, I was shocked one day when I was transferred directly to Carlos. "Ar-ly'-nnn, how nice to hear from you," he barely whispered, "How are you on this magnificent day?" I could hear the heavy downbeat of '70s disco music in the background, uncommon for a doctor's office. We chatted about our lesson that evening, after his office hours. He confirmed "yes," he had completed the assignment in preparation and "yes," he had totaled the hours in his logbook as we were in final prep for the checkride. After several minutes, sounding disappointed, he stated that he needed to go—he was in the middle of performing surgery! He ended with, "I look forward to seeing you tonight." He was even more charming than his son.

The Rockwell 114TC is a single-engine aircraft with a wide cockpit and generous bucket seats. Fine detailing and artisanship gives the look of an expensive automobile rather than an airplane. Carlos's 114 had an N-number that included his initials. She was a low-wing that sat on tall, retractable-gear legs and she groaned under his heft as he climbed atop the wing and slid into the pilot seat.

The air was smooth and the stars were bright for our final tweak of ILS IAPs. Carlos and I had been concerned about the engine sounding rough and occasionally missing, so I was glad to know that the maintenance shop had recently looked her over in anticipation of our night flight.

We had just crossed the final approach fix; the outer-marker beacon was winding down. Carlos had just extended the gear and retarded the throttle to begin descent. Under the hood, he was busy with the many tasks over the marker. With everything else going on, he showed no reaction when the engine RPM, without warning, went to something near zero. "Your airplane, my throttle," I announced. It's a command I often give to students when practicing simulated engine failures so it was a familiar one for Carlos to hear.

I reacted, stretching my body across the center storage console and lay over his right leg. I placed my left elbow on the front edge of the seat, between his legs, to steady myself while my fingers twisted the ignition key directly below the yoke. My right hand was on the throttle, poised for the engine restart attempt. About this time, I felt Carlos's right hand on my side, at my waist. His hand gave a little squeeze. "Ar-ly'-nnn, not now," I heard in my headset.

Yes, we were on final descent with the runway straight ahead, but I didn't see any reason to delay engine re-start procedures and I said, "Why not now?"

I became vaguely aware that his hand had moved down, his arm outstretched on my thigh. He gave a small squeeze. "Let's wait until we get on the ground."

I didn't think we would make the runway from our present position without the engine. "Why? I'd like to have it now."

He squealed with delight and purred my name in the way that only Carlos could.

About then the engine jumped back to life. I sat up and quickly reassessed our altitude and position, having not been able to see over the instrument panel while my head was near Carlos's lap. "I liked that!" I heard in my headset, "Please, feel free to do that again anytime!" I was happy that Carlos appreciated my quick actions to restart his engine.

We were fine; our glidepath had barely slipped below glideslope. Carlos's ILS procedures were top-notch; he wasn't even stressed out. It made me feel accomplished as an instructor that Carlos was so well trained that he could handle a distraction like an engine failure without missing a beat. "Your technique, sir, is exquisite!" I complimented. He squealed with delight.

However, the engine was still "not right" and when he made another throttle reduction on short final the engine finally groaned and died. We were only about 300 feet AGL but with the runway now safely made, I wasn't concerned. Carlos lifted his hood at decision altitude and made a beautiful, full-stall touchdown with almost no roll out. We stopped with little braking.

Still on the runway, I decided to attempt a restart so we'd be able to taxi clear. Once again, I stretched over, lying on Carlos's leg, my elbow again between his legs while I twisted the ignition key. Carlos seemed excited to finally be on the ground. "Ar-ly'-nnn, shall I call us someplace?" *Huh?*

It must be his accent; at times, I didn't grasp exactly what Carlos said. "Carlos, call UNICOM and get them to send out a tug. We're gonna need to be towed in, I can't get her started."

*Tug?* Now *he* seemed confused.... "The engine is dead? When did that happen?" He was just now becoming fully aware of our situation.

"When she died the first time, over the marker, I was able to restart her. But now I think she's a goner."

We shut down the avionics, flipped off the master, and waited for the tug. It was very still and quiet sitting on the runway. "Ar-ly'nnn, I am so embarrassed," he said with only the faint runway lights illuminating the cockpit. "There's no reason to be embarrassed, an engine failure is no reflection on you," I reassured him.

Carlos's voice was soft. He spoke with the sadness of a doctor informing his patient about the results of a poor cancer screening. He confided to having fantasized about us. He confessed that he thought, he hoped, he imagined that we would be together, after landing tonight. *Call me clueless, I had no idea!*

I waited until we had returned to the harsh and bright lights of the flight school and with several people around. Instead of leading Carlos to the busy classroom, we went to a semi-private corner. This post-flight review required privacy.

I assured Carlos that he was a desirable man but reminded him that I had gone to school with his son. I told him that he was deserving of every kind word I'd ever given him but that he must not misinterpret my intentions. My affection toward him was as a father figure. I made certain he knew that I was happy being his instructor and I hoped he would allow me to continue in that role. He nodded and we hugged; it was over. We never spoke of it again.

He continued to fly with me for many years following his instrument practical exam for flight reviews, IPCs and anytime he felt skills becoming rusty. We enjoyed a close friendship.

Carlos was the first client of mine who became amorous but I was no longer naive. I've received flowers, gifts, and more than one marriage proposal from clients. It's not that I was a beauty queen—far from it. They weren't being dastardly men nor were they sexist pigs. It's just easy for people of either sex to become infatuated with their flight instructor.

If a flight instructor carries out the job well, the student benefits. Think about it. Ordinary people don't regularly receive praise the way a student does from a good instructor. Most people don't forge personal relationships steeped in respect and trust the way an instructor does with a student. People don't feel accomplishment or self-actualization in their daily life the way a well-taught student does.

It's easy for a student to associate those pleasant feelings with the instructor rather than with the job the instructor is performing. Combine that with the closeness of the cockpit and a few late night appointments and you have conditions primed for men and women to think about what men and women do.... *Geez*, even I fell in love and married *my* flight instructor!

...

As a side note, unwanted sexual advances make exciting headline news. If it should happen to you, only you can decide if what you experienced was an assault or the warm feelings generated by a good student/instructor relationship. Give thought to how you will deflect an unwanted advance from a customer when it is something innocent. If you plan for it ahead of time, you can do it gracefully, without escalating it into something bigger and without hurt feelings. You can preserve a client and their ego. You will feel proud of yourself for having done it right.

Oh, and one more thing: I recommend calling, texting or sending emails to clients a day or so before a lesson. If they haven't had time to complete an assignment, such as planning a cross-country NavLog, it may affect the lesson. At least you'll know in advance and have time to tweak how to spend wisely the customer's time. It also helps to remind those who may be inclined to no-show.

**Read more about these concepts in the *Aviation Instructor's Handbook:***

Listening

Getting emotional rather than listening

Barriers to effective communication

Making assumptions

# stories about

## the teaching process

I received an instrument rating when NDB approaches were part of the practical exam. NDBs were my nemesis. I probably logged 100 hours learning the dang things, which cost me thousands of dollars. I haven't shot an NDB approach in twenty years.

There was a time when I considered getting out of flight instruction. It appeared that nothing ever changed. I taught the same stuff, the same way, for decades. The industry was stagnant and I was bored. Then suddenly it was as though someone flipped a switch and things started moving. Then it began racing, challenging me to keep up with all the changes. I lost sleep learning GPS the week before I had to teach it to a student. Instructors who graduated last year are learning ADS-B as new information and who knows what new technology or system is next to come down the pipe.

Learning can't be just facts when the facts won't matter tomorrow or don't yet exist. Our teaching process must teach students how to learn. When access to information was limited, we needed to load students up with facts. Now, with quick access to every fact, we must equip them with the understanding to solve problems. They need critical thinking skills to know which online resources and spokesmen to trust. The goal must be to fill the industry with lifetime learners, not simply graduates.

Our teaching process must instill respect for the system. Aviation is very much on the honor-code. Seldom are the number of hours recorded in a logbook questioned and there is no traffic cop sitting behind the cloud with a measuring tape. Our system is wholly dependent on the integrity of individual pilots.

In this chapter, you'll read stories about getting the student's attention and in making the lessons stick.

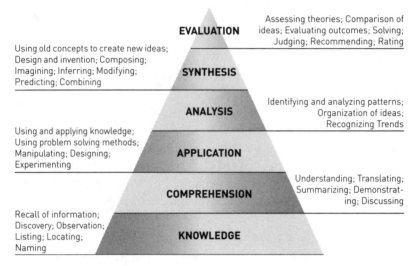

**Figure 4-1.** Higher order thinking skills (HOTS) lie in the last three categories of Bloom's Taxonomy of Learning: analysis, synthesis and evaluation skills.

# An Exercise

Let's try an exercise. We'll plan a lesson. Plan to teach something simple—something you know how to do without needing any research. Consider taxiing. You know how to taxi, right? It's one of the earliest procedures a new pilot learns. You've done it hundreds of time, I'm certain. So off the top of your head, make a list of everything a pilot needs to know to taxi from the ramp area to the active runway at your airport. Go ahead, I'll wait….

This is the way I start every instructor ground school. The discussion that follows often becomes rowdy as class participants recall more and more elements to add to the growing list on the whiteboard. No one person can think of them all. As a class, they usually get most of them, but when we do the research, we still identify three or four items not on the whiteboard that should've been.

It's a great demonstration in why a professional flight instructor always uses a prepared lesson plan. A new pilot needs more content than we, as experienced pilots, first realize. It's difficult to remember a time when we didn't know how to taxi and that makes it difficult to relate to the level of detail that our students need. Any instructor can easily remember the obvious items, but not too many can remember the finer details without a lesson plan.

Don't worry too much over the format of a lesson plan. It only needs to be something useful to you. Lesson plans are not something that you spend hours creating for passing a test, only to be filed in a three-ring binder and put on the shelf. To a professional, these are working documents, which you'll likely revise several times, even after you've been certificated, as you continue to hone your craft.

After you have a complete list of items to cover, did you remember to define for your student what you mean by the term "taxi"? Don't forget the obvious! Did you tell the student why he wants to pay you to learn to do this thing—what is his motivation? Did you tell the student a funny story, something to get his attention?

> At KLEX, the only taxiway between the ramp and runway circles the airline terminal ramp. The airlines use orange highway cones to segregate areas and to mark pedestrian aisles for passengers walking from the terminal to the planes. There must be hundreds of orange cones sitting on the airline ramp at one time. One day, a great breeze blew through unexpectedly. I was sitting at the run-up area, preparing for takeoff, when it blew up and I decided it best to return to the ramp rather than to fly. Well, you can imagine my taxi back to the flight school trying to dodge orange cones that had blown all over the taxiway. Many times, I had to stop right in the middle of the taxiway, turning the airplane into the wind, while I waited for cones to be moved—either by the wind or by ground personnel—before I could continue. What a fiasco!

Did that little story get your attention? Which elements will we likely discuss after that? For starters, that it is OK to abort a flight when something unexpected, like weather, happens. All takeoffs are optional, as they say. The reasoning and decision behind stopping and turning into the wind is a concept too often overlooked. The importance of carefulness when negotiating around foreign objects, debris, and people near the plane should be included. These are each items that speak to decision-making and risk management. A story, even about something as routine as taxiing, turns a mundane procedure into something exciting and worth learning. You can teach more than just textbook-related test material. Teach how to think about and how to use the material.

**Read more about these concepts in the *Aviation Instructor's Handbook:***

Presentation of a Lesson

Attention

Motivation

# Dick

I met Dick in a bar. It was a party for a friend. Someone brought Dick to the party and introduced us. His voice boomed when the crowd helped the band in singing *Friends in Low Places*. A modern-day combination of Ernest Hemingway and Indiana Jones, Dick lived life to the fullest. He relayed experiences about whitewater rafting on wild rivers, snow skiing atop frigid mountains, and SCUBA diving among bizarre sea creatures. Leaving the party, I thought to myself that if even a small fraction of those stories were true, this man had lived an amazingly exciting life. His stories inspired me to live like that.

Before meeting Dick, I thought stories were a boring penance that a small child had to endure when unable to escape grandpa's lap. However, Dick's stories were rich; they were vivid and memorable. Long after he shared a tale, I would find myself replaying it in my mind, contemplating different aspects. I even retold them to friends, enjoying them again. His were more than a punch line; they added flavor and texture to life.

We became friends. I taught him to fly and Dick schooled me in how to weave a great tale. I just sat back and listened in awe. He added to whatever subject we were discussing. If the topic of conversation was weather, his story probably involved temperatures at one extreme or another, or a beautiful rainbow he'd seen during some blue water ocean voyage. His story always included something interesting. Perhaps it was a new idea I wanted to remember or maybe there was something unexpected. Regardless, his stories were intense. I actually felt for whoever the character was. Dick gave me the biggest belly laughs and at other times scared me to death. I loved that his words could make me *feel* like that, to evoke my emotions.

I began to wonder if a relevant, well-told, intense story could help students learn such boring aviation topics as regulations, risk management, and fundamentals of instructing.

My poor ground school participants; they learned in spite of me putting them to sleep. For years, I built boring, business-as-usual PowerPoint presentations for students that even I didn't want to watch. Why did I do that? I love to read stories and watch movies. I was in Toastmaster's competitions. I was a story consumer, but failed to recognize the power of storytelling to assist the teaching process. I vowed to move beyond death-by-PowerPoint bullets to harness a well-told parable.

Slowly, I started collecting and sharing the happenings in my life. Usually, they were replays about experiences flying in icing conditions or near a thunderstorm—something I should not have been doing. My poor ground school class; as a captive audience, there was no place for them to flee while I practiced my new technique. If they were wise enough to learn from my mistakes, then my graduates were armed for success. After years of flying, I had plenty of mistake material. I hoped that they would find a valuable takeaway in a tale that illustrated my PowerPoint slide.

I decided that if a story could validate what I was teaching, then it had purpose and it was worthwhile. If I could give an example of one way out of the problem by sharing how I handled my situation, then it had training value. In addition, if by sharing my mistakes it prevented another pilot from doing the same, then it had all the ingredients for a successful training experience.

The age-old tradition of sitting around the FBO lobby and telling flying stories, known as hangar flying, is all but gone. That's a shame. Telling stories is not merely an intellectual exercise. They are personal experiences. Sharing stories is a way to touch people and to connect with them emotionally. More importantly, this can help pilots remember and apply lessons in ways that simple checklists can't.

Long after training is complete, long after the student has forgotten your name, your face, or the sound of your voice, he will remember the story. Stories have impact. Even today, my graduates from decades ago tell me, "I always remember the one you told about…" I'm amazed at how well they retain not only the concept but also details with amazing clarity. Maya Angelou said, "People will forget what you said and they will forget what you did, but they will never forget how you made them feel." What's the best way to make people feel something? Tell them a great story.

Scientific work has identified how a relevant story told with intensity and inspiring feeling can affect our attitudes, beliefs, and behaviors.[1] Even after the story ends, the feelings or behaviors of its characters continue to resonate with us. It explains the pep in your step after a feel-good movie, why you remember the chorus line to a song, and why I am motivated to head to the gym after watching any movie starring Catherine Zeta-Jones.

A word of caution, though: keep your stories current. I've had to retire stories about W0X0F[2], ADF approaches[3], and DF steers[4]. Never heard of these? That's my point exactly. These technologies from yesteryear aren't relevant to a student learning to fly today.

Soon, I'll have to retire stories about paper charts—the ones about students shredding their sectionals after getting tied up trying to refold them in the cockpit, and the bound approach IAPs sliding out of reach on the cockpit floor. As GPS continues to dominate navigation, I'll soon have to discard VOR stories, and how we become dyslexic trying to navigate on the 300, 330, 003 and 030 radials.

**Read more about these concepts in the *Aviation Instructor's Handbook*:**

Concept learning

Law of effect

Law of intensity

Teaching process

Performance-based objectives

Scenario-based training

Decision-making objectives

Presentation of a lesson

...

My greatest achievement came a few years back. After an upbeat and energetic ground school class with several of my better-rehearsed tales, a student came forward to thank me. He enjoyed the class... meaning that he hadn't fallen asleep. He said, "I don't know, but if even a small number of your stories are true you have lived an awesome life!" He seemed surprised when I gave him a big hug.

1   Paul J. Zak, "How Stories Change the Brain," *Greater Good* e-newsletter (University of California, December 17, 2013). Accessed January 24, 2016. http://greatergood.berkeley.edu/article/item/how_stories_change_brain

2   Weather reports coming off teletype machines were abbreviated, similar to today's METARS and TAFs. "W0X0F" was the abbreviation for "indefinite zero ceiling obscured; zero visibility, fog." In other words, a really nasty day for flying; but because it was pronounceable it made for really good stories.

3   The Automatic Direction Finder (ADF) was far from that. When used during a non-precision instrument approach, this instrument required the pilot to calculate bearings, almost causing at least one blond pilot of my close acquaintance to quit flying altogether.

4   Flight Service Stations used to have direction-finding equipment so that when a pilot transmitted on a specific frequency, the meteorologist could "find" the plane's position on a simple radar-type screen. The meteorologist could then give the pilot a heading to steer to the FSS, thus the name "a direction-finding-steer" (or DF Steer). Its intent, as far as I was concerned, was to help a young pilot find her way home.

# Kerry

Twice, Kerry had failed an initial flight instructor practical exam and now he was looking for someone to prepare him for a third attempt. He was a mature, experienced schoolteacher. He considered himself an educator. Additionally, he was a seasoned pilot with a healthy-sized logbook and therefore assumed that he knew what was important in making safe pilots. With his background, he was shocked to find himself not yet a certificated flight instructor.

Kerry felt that aviation in his area, including instructors, examiners and FAA inspectors, was a rich man's country club. On his small teacher's pay, he didn't feel welcome in that group. From his perspective, he was mistreated and mishandled. He was angry at the whole pilot-certification process. He didn't believe he'd been given a fair chance. In short, he had a lot of emotional baggage. For all of these reasons, he chose to travel from Louisiana to my school, escaping into a new area— one he hoped would be accepting of him.

He agreed to my price for a four-hour evaluation, which would be the basis of making a polish-up plan. I emailed three assignments for him to prepare ahead of time:

1. Present an introductory lecture on steep turns; a maneuver briefing as you would deliver it to a student.

2. Case study: Using the Suzy Sample student logbook that I provided, make a list of what is required by regulation in order for Suzy to earn a recommendation for an FAA private pilot practical exam.

3. In the plane, teach me engine start, run-up and taxi to the active runway. We're not flying. We'll be on the ground but in the plane and in motion.

My evaluation of Kerry began the minute he blew through the door, a laptop bag slung sloppily over one shoulder with a jacket dragging on the floor. His fully loaded backpack threatened every seam. In one hand, he barely carried an overstuffed flight bag. The other hand coaxed along a UPS-style hand truck with two overflowing plastic bins whose lids couldn't close and an oversized cardboard box topping the stack. The hefty load was unbalanced and gave every appearance of tipping into a great mess. He was twenty minutes late.

His hair was long and in dreadlocks. It was all over his face so he could barely see to walk, and with both hands full, he couldn't clear a view. He was overloaded and disheveled. Several staff members, seeing him appearing so, rushed to his rescue. I could only sit there, amazed and amused.

After some effort, we finally got Kerry "moved in" to our little meeting corner. With all of his stuff packed against the wall there was barely room to walk around the table. I gave him a few minutes to settle in and catch his breath. After staff introductions, a facility tour, and answers to a few questions, it was time to get to work. "Take ten minutes, prepare to introduce me to steep turns, and I'll be back with some water for us."

Returning to Kerry, I found no space on the tabletop to sit two bottles of water. He had a humongous three-ring binder laid open, with ragged corners of loose paper sticking out from all sides. Several different toy airplanes sat, ready for simulated flight. A small stack of books was here and more papers covered the rest of the table over there. It felt cluttered, almost overwhelming. I handed him a bottle of water and sat mine on the floor. Then I waited to be dazzled.

His presentation was not instructional. Nothing was clear, concise, correct or complete. His talk was all over the place. Tangents of thought weaved a great web, without any clear direction on how to perform a steep turn. In spite of everything, many of the required elements were completely missing.

The presentation had taken more than an hour. He often stopped to search for references from this box or that. His references weren't training aids to benefit the student; they were crutches to supplement holes in his knowledge. Nevertheless, for all the effort put into lugging hordes of material, nothing was organized enough to be usable. I was stunned that anyone would have endorsed him for a checkride—not once, but twice.

Kerry was passionate about aviation. He was warm and charming. He possessed plenty of people skills, but not the subject matter expertise. He didn't control his time, and management and assessment skills were also missing. I was gentle in my critique; he was defensive. I focused on details; he became angry. I pulled out the PTS. He pulled out the race card.

Without warning, Kerry stood so fast that the chair was sent toppling backwards. He spoke loudly, as if needing to attract attention, insisting that this treatment was unfair because he was black. With that, he stomped off. I could only sit there, in shock.

A short time later, he returned. When I asked if he wished to continue, Kerry said, "Only if you're gonna be nice." He had asked for an assessment. If that's what he still wanted, then no, I wasn't going to be nice, at least not how he defined the term. To be effective, I had to say what needed saying. I would do it thoughtfully and with compassion, but if his goal was to improve, then he needed to hear a specific, constructive critique.

Kerry agreed to continue with a review of the logbook problem. Suzy Sample would have been in a heap of trouble with Kerry as her instructor. Suzy's logbook was lacking in several obvious ways that Kerry had missed, but I didn't say that. Instead, I opened the FARs and showed him.

"Did Suzy meet that requirement?"

"No."

"Is Suzy eligible for an endorsement?"

"No."

"Did we include it on our to-do list for Suzy?"

"No," and with that, he stomped off again. Kerry didn't need me to say that he'd not done well on this exercise, either.

Upon his return, he talked about how difficult it had been for him to earn pilot certificates. He had to count his pennies carefully. Financial obligations interrupted his training on several occasions. He'd had several instructors leave, thus causing him to repeat lessons and spend money ramping up with a new replacement. I let him vent for another few minutes before I offered, "I'm sorry that happened to you but I can't go back and fix that. I can only assure that things are done correctly going forward."

People hang on to emotional baggage and for some reason they want to share it. We could have sat for an extensive rehashing of the past, but I prefer to keep customers focused on here and now. My focus was on how my training techniques would differ from what he had experienced in the past.

I thought things might be better in the plane. They weren't. In the plane, Kerry tended to speak in very long sentences, lecturing me on this or that as if we were sitting in the chair back at the flight school office, rather than in a moving bucket of bolts. This forced me to choose whether to distract my attention away from flying to listen to what he was explaining to me, or to stop listening so I could handle the various tasks needed to maneuver the plane. *Whew!*

He needed to speak like this. Short sentences. Small thoughts. Like training a puppy. Sit. Stay. Lay down. Roll over. In the plane, limit your words. Say what to do. Don't lecture. Learn it on the ground. Do it in the plane. Teach using short, action statements. Beginning students don't multitask well. Don't make them choose between listening and flying.

Kerry had an inflated view of his skill set. It wasn't arrogance. He *was* a teacher and therefore thought the title of flight instructor was a shoe-in. From his perspective, there was no other explanation about why he wasn't a flight instructor other than the "rich folks" in his area didn't accept him. They probably didn't—but not because of his race or socioeconomic status. He had not yet developed the knowledge and skill to be an effective flight instructor.

I love objective testing standards. They are clear, concise, complete and correct—the 4Cs of an effective instructor. It was easy to have Kerry look at the objective completion requirements listed in the testing standards and decide for himself if he met the criteria.

When working with student pilots I might sugarcoat words, being careful not to overly excite or engender fear on their part. However, for higher-level candidates—especially when preparing for graduation— the gloves come off. As they say in the Navy Seals, "There are only two ways to do something: the right away, and again." He'd already done it again. How did Kerry want to proceed now?

In my opinion, Kerry had received inadequate instruction, but not for the reasons he believed. Kerry was a difficult case. He was head-strong, defensive, and opinionated. He did not accept criticism well and became belligerent when informed he was in error. When he ran out of excuses, he became irrational and emotional. Learning to fly is an emotional roller coaster sure to spark every emotion across the human spectrum. For Kerry, it took time to learn to even out the emotional peaks and valleys.

I suspect his previous instructor had simply given up. He didn't want to address the issues. It was easier to allow the FAA to fail him. Maybe Kerry didn't have a professional mindset because the instructor wasn't a good example.

Kerry returned home with a mission to use a voice recorder and email each maneuver briefing. In that way, we could work together long-distance. After listening to his recordings, I called him to dis-cuss problems and suggest refinements. We found that software such as GoToMeeting.com allowed us to share documents, and he could view my ground school PowerPoints. It was a very effective way to work together on ground knowledge and teaching style. The monthly fee for the software was far cheaper than the drive and motel expenses.

Kerry required more than just polish and it took several months. It was difficult to bring him down gently, without damaging his ego, but I needed him to reset his self-perception. He called me cold, cruel, heartless and stoic. He accused me of trying to change his basic personality. In some ways I was.

He showed up for one of our face-to-face appointments with a pair of glasses. His "flight instructor glasses" were like a cape, transforming Kerry into Super Instructor; and in that role, he allowed himself to walk and talk in a way that was different from his natural self. It wasn't a change in his personality but more like an actor cast in a scene. It worked. Super Instructor was born.

Although Kerry became angry with me and quit several times, he always came back. He saw that I was not giving up on him. He knew that I wouldn't lower the criterion and that bullying me would not result in a premature sign-off for his checkride. If and when I signed him off, it would be with my full belief that he would pass. I respected his tenacity.

Kerry slowly transformed into a clear-thinking, concise-speaking professional with no need for more than a small roller bag of reference materials. I presented him with the option of retesting with the FSDO in my area or in his area. I hoped he would retest at home. It was important for Kerry to pass his checkride in his area—with the people who he thought did not accept him. I was confident that they would be proud to have Kerry, now an aviation professional, in their community.

He passed with his local FSDO.

**Read more about these concepts in the *Aviation Instructor's Handbook*:**

Teaching skills

Criteria

The importance of PTS in training

Organization of material

Lecture methods

Case study method

Electronic learning

Instructional aids

# 5

stories
about
## assessment

The purpose of assessment is improvement. Like a used car, we accept the customer "as is; where is" and we help to move him forward in his goals. We assess his current status, what is needed, and then we continue assessing along the way to stay on course.

What students need most is an honest assessment, but sometimes the assessment is not accurate. Being kind to student feelings or instructor complacency does not serve the best interest of the customer. In these cases, hopefully, another instructor will catch it and get the client back on track.

In this chapter, you'll read accounts of inaccurate assessments and what was needed to benefit the customer.

| | DESCRIBE | EXPLAIN | PRACTICE | PERFORM |
|---|---|---|---|---|
| Steep Turns / Slow Flight / Stalls / Emergencies | Pilot can describe physical characteristics/cognitive elements of the maneuver. | Pilot can explain the maneuver's underlying concepts, principles, and procedures. | Pilot can plan and execute the maneuvers with coaching and assistance to correct deviations and errors. | Pilot can plan and execute the maneuver to PTS standards without assistance or coaching. Pilot identifies and corrects errors and deviations. |

**Figure 5-1.** Rubric for assessing flight training maneuvers. (FAA)

# Don

Dear Arlynn,

I've just been promoted to Assistant Chief Instructor. I am now the primary check airman for students in the private pilot course but I'm finding it difficult to fail people. Is there a nice way to do it? I just hate failing students. I remember how nervous I was and how I dreaded every Prog Check. I don't want the students in my school to have that experience. Is there a way to make it a positive experience? Thanks in advance,

Don

Hi Don,

Thanks for emailing and giving me a chance to share my opinion. Let me start with a quick story.

A few years back, my oldest, dearest, bestest friend in the world enrolled in flight training at my school. When the day came that I had to fail him on a Prog Check, I was heartbroken. I carefully chose what to say and how to say it so as not to hurt his feelings or our friendship.

When the other students found out that Best Friend had failed, they were horrified. They assumed that if I was calloused enough to fail even my good buddy, surely it was proof that they had no hope of passing. Even the staff was stunned. Suddenly, whisperings in the hall were hushed and groups surrounding the coffeepot dispersed when I passed by. I already had a reputation for being tough; now I had graduated to monster.

They didn't understand that it was precisely because he was my very dear friend that I failed him. I wanted my friend's training experience to be effective so that his piloting experience would be successful. The interesting thing was that Best Friend was not surprised about failing. He would not expect me to allow his major infractions to slide. He wanted to be a good pilot and he was counting on me to make him just that.

This may sound strange, but you have to convince the student that it is in their best interest to go back for a tad more polish. Years from now, they won't remember the results of this Prog Check, but they will always remember their successful FAA practical exam because of what they learned along the way, during the Prog evaluations. Make their highest priority not about passing the Prog Check, but in becoming a safe pilot. The Prog Check is only one small step along that path.

Try not to use the f-word (failure); focus on the standards and that the student hasn't *yet* met the measure. Try to be constructive in your evaluation, with specifics on how to improve. Make sure the student knows that you're looking forward to passing them on the retest.

Now, for ideas on how to make it a positive experience, here are a few that have worked for me:

1. Be accessible before the Prog Check so that students feel they can ask questions. Sometimes it's helpful for them to meet you before the evaluation.

2. During the preflight briefing, review the performance expectations. If the Prog Check does not use the testing standard for certification as the criterion, as is common in earlier checks, then be sure to publish benchmarks. Students should not be guessing "what you want." They want to know what is expected before flight. If this is an evaluation with a one-time-only-attempt at a maneuver, as is the case in later checks, be sure to inform the student before getting to the plane. Confirm that the student feels prepared to meet the standard and be willing to reschedule if there are doubts. On cross-countries, I would say something like, "I expect you to be on course, with our first checkpoint identified and an ETA calculated for our next checkpoint, within twenty miles." With that, the student can make any needed adjustments to his planning before getting to the plane.

3. When it's bad, tell them in the air. If for whatever reason the flight was unsatisfactory, tell them immediately, while their performance is still fresh in their mind. Be specific. If it was a bust on heading and altitude or on a procedure, let them know right away. Don't let them get all the way back to the classroom table and then surprise them with an unsatisfactory during the debrief. That opens the possibility that the student will remember something different from you.

4. When it's a pass, tell the whole world, but when it's not, keep it confidential. Preserve their ego. Be sympathetic but not apologetic.

5. During the debrief, have a nice balance of what went right and what needs to change. It doesn't have to be 50/50, but surely there were a few good things that will make the assessment feel fair and acceptable. Don't flatter them with insincerities. Praise them on specific tasks done well.

6. I like to organize my debriefings as a replay of the flight. That way the student knows their performance is the focus and not them. The topic of discussion is always the performance and not the person.

7. Allow them to tell their side of the story. Listen to what they want to say. Encourage them to express their opinion. Sometimes I find that students do the wrong things but for the right reasons. Be prepared to salute their thought process even if the outcome didn't shine.

8. On later Prog Checks, as they are nearing graduation, allow the student to assess himself. This has a benefit of teaching the pilot to assess his performance. In this way, we create graduates who continue to learn. A pilot should learn to evaluate his proficiency so he recognizes when he needs additional training.

I recall one particular student who did not pass a Prog Check because of his simulated engine failure procedure. In my mind, this is an important task. Of all the things a pilot learns, this one has the potential to save lives. This guy could not successfully glide to a field despite having three tries. The instructors worked on him for four hours before sending him back.

He passed the Prog Check retest but then, on his FAA practical exam, he was again unsatisfactory because of the same thing. The examiner sent him back and the instructors worked on him another three hours before sending him for a retest. He passed.

It was the second flight after passing his FAA practical exam. He was returning home, after dark, at 3,000 feet AGL in a C172 when the engine quit. It was a catastrophic engine failure. He successfully glided to the NRST airport shown on the GPS moving map. First thing the next morning, he called the school to thank everyone for failing him and for helping him to improve his technique. That's what it's all about: the happy conclusion to the story.

Passing students is easy. Failing them is difficult because of the emotional baggage attached. Nevertheless, if you know in your heart that you evaluated them objectively then don't feel badly. Don't feel guilty, and never apologize for failing someone; you might be saving their life.

I hope that helps! Congrats on the promotion.

Arlynn

...

Now, readers, maybe you are the instructor whose student has just failed a Prog Check or a practical exam. It is counterproductive to belittle the training system, the completion standards, or the evaluator. I know some instructors think this is a way to befriend students, but your students aren't paying you to be their friend. Support the system and the standards for safety sake. Turn it into a positive learning experience for them.

**Read more about these concepts in the** *Aviation Instructor's Handbook:*

General characteristics of an effective assessment

# Megan

With milk-white skin, red hair and emerald eyes, Megan was the kind of gal that men fawned over. She dressed to feature prominently her generous feminine assets. Her lightweight skirts always caught the faintest breeze while she teetered on the strut, checking the fuel. It wasn't her that I disliked; it was the way she made every man go stupid when she flashed her beauty-queen smile.

Instructors fell all over themselves to fly with her. They would line up at the lobby windows overlooking the ramp to watch her preflight. They waited patiently for her return so they could be among the first to jog out and assist with securing the plane. Often I would see a team—a different instructor at each tie-down while still another found enough courtesy to carry her feather-light flight bag into the office. They melted when she purred, "Why, thank you *soo* much." It was disturbing to see testosterone poisoning at full strength and I'm quite certain that I mentioned it to the staff, on more than one occasion.

It appeared to me that her single goal in life was to completely disrupt the otherwise efficient operations at my flight school. I could find no potion to cure the spell she cast. When I saw her on my schedule for a Prog Check after lunch, I desperately searched for any excuse to cancel but could find none.

Passing this Prog Check meant that she would be eligible to solo, so I carefully reviewed her training record. She had flown with six different instructors. *Hmm*, that was a red flag. She had passed a prior Prog Check on the first attempt; however, she required three attempts before passing her pre-solo knowledge exam. Another red flag. I asked her a few questions regarding the areas found deficient, enough to reveal that she *still* had not properly grasped the needed knowledge. That was a third red flag. As a rule, I would have called the Prog Check unsuccessful and ended it there. Nevertheless, knowing that everyone around was aware of how I felt about her, I wanted to battle any possible perception of bias or jealousy toward the pretty student.

In the plane, I found her radio skills lacking and asked her about it. She informed me that, unlike me, the other instructors were willing to help her. This was not the norm. Students were normally managing radio work by the fourth or fifth hour, needing assistance only during non-routine situations.

Megan's approaches were not up to par. She was inconsistent in her glidepath—one time too high, the next too low—and she allowed her airspeed to vary widely. I quizzed her about this and again I was curtly informed that the instructors were much nicer than I—meaning they were willing to lend assistance. I was seeing a trend.

Back on the ramp, I could see the line of noses pressed to the windows as Megan shut down the engine. The barrage of instructors rushing from the door toward the plane meant that they were jogging out to help us—um, *her*—secure the plane. I quickly got out and, facing the oncoming stampede, held my hand up in a "stop" signal. Small clouds of dust formed around their feet as they slid to a halt. I redirected them back inside.

Returning to Megan, I requested her to secure the plane and stood back to watch. She begged for help and began to cry. She didn't know how to connect the towbar to the C172 nose; she didn't know where to push it or how to maneuver it by hand. She let me know how my customer service was lacking in comparison to the rest of my staff. She assumed that I was simply being cruel and that she would fail her Prog Check because I didn't like her.

I had her stand back and watch me, another female, maneuver the plane by hand into the tie-down. No excuses. Once the plane was in place, the demonstration complete, I pulled it back out of the parking spot and beckoned her to do it. She required instruction and a lot of persuading. After much pouting and effort, she was successful and a little more than proud of the result.

She knew nothing about how to tie a proper non-slip knot. Again, I demonstrated, then untied it and motioned for her to do it. It took a few tries but, with encouragement, we were both satisfied with the final result. I flashed her a big smile.

I found her willing to learn, once she understood the importance of being self-sufficient. During the debrief we talked about single-pilot resource management and she seemed to get it. I explained that she was not ready to solo because she still required assistance on many tasks. I wasn't being mean; I was insistent that she act as the pilot-in-command. I suggested she had to bridle the men around her. She must inform instructors that she did not desire them to be overly helpful and that she wanted them to teach *her* to handle each task. "Even parking the plane?" she whined, still perspiring from her recent effort. "Until you can park it solo, you can't fly it solo," I replied. It wasn't the answer she hoped for, but she seemed to find it fair.

Even though the Prog Check was not successful, she seemed content and appreciative of all that she'd learned. I was disappointed in my staff, however. In my opinion, she had not received adequate instruction.

The instructors had treated Megan as a fragile princess. They were taking care of her rather than grooming her to become an independent, self-sufficient pilot. By being overly helpful, instructors had robbed her of the opportunity to succeed. Students require these small successes to build confidence. Maslow's pinnacle of basic needs, self-actualization, will never be attained without effort and hard work.

Instructors weren't inspiring her to take control as pilot-in-command. The result was that she had no perception of what that term really meant. Pilot-*in-command*—in-command; in-charge; in-control; and making the decisions. This isn't a natural trait for most people. We must teach it, they must learn it, and we must practice it. Students will naturally slip up in their early attempts and will require careful instructor oversight until mastered.

...

Here are a few concepts in this story that warrant focus:

1. We all have personal biases. Eventually you will be matched with a client that for some reason you don't like. Be honest with yourself about the types of people you don't like. Do you believe fat people are lazy? Do you think that Democrats are stupid or that a woman's place is in the home? We'd all like to think we could set our feelings aside and do the job. In real life, it's not so easy. You'll have to choose what you consider a professional way to handle it. You might be doing the client a favor if you can pass him or her along to a different instructor.

2. Women cry. There, I've said it. I know, *I know*, it's not a politically correct thing to say. I'm not being sexist; I'm simply stating 30 years' experience as a flight instructor. We sometimes cry when we get angry or frustrated or because we are disappointed. Without fail, me included, every female student in my flight school cried at some point during flight training. Most men are not comfortable with a woman's tears. If you're a male instructor teaching a female client, this can cause a problem. My word of advice is to have a frank discussion with your mother or other female confidant to give you ideas on how best to handle a female in tears.

**Read more about these concepts in the *Aviation Instructor's Handbook:***

Learning from error

Purpose of assessment

Authentic assessment

# Chase

According to Oscar Wilde, "Some cause happiness wherever they go; others, whenever they go." Chase was the latter. He was different, in a peculiar sort of way. His mannerisms made him less than enjoyable to have around. He was an odd-duck. Besides a small eye-twitching tick, there was nothing in particular to point to as being off; he was just a very strange-acting fella.

Despite having been involved in training for a couple of years and accumulating way too many hours, he was not yet a pilot. His logbook was unusual with several items that were not as I would expect. When I asked Chase about specific entries, he was quick to say that his current log was a re-creation from a lost one. A few minutes later when I asked about a particular line item, he had a different explanation. I thought this odd.

In general, he talked too much, too fast, and offered too many justifications. It didn't feel right. The more I contemplated, the more I was convinced that this training record was a total fabrication.

Students engaged in training normally depart from the same airport for each lesson. His training didn't. Dual lessons weren't properly endorsed. As an instructor, you know the sequence to introduce maneuvers. His log recorded steep turns on lesson number one and other slight anomalies. With the Internet, it's easy to locate airports by their identifiers and get a sense of the geographic location of cross-country destinations. His didn't make sense. Considering an approximate speed of a given airplane, it's easy to estimate if the hours logged on a cross-country are reasonable. His didn't come close. Other entries were simply ineligible. *If it doesn't walk like a duck or quack like a duck...*

I voiced "concern" about his records. I pointed out "potential problems" with the way his previous instructors recorded apparent training. I stopped short of coming straight out and saying the word *fraudulent*. However, I made copies and took hordes of notes during my initial assessment.

The FSDO needed to be involved with Chase, so I called them but I didn't see any evidence that they were going to do anything. Meanwhile, I saw no reason why we couldn't give Chase the training that he needed, so I enrolled him. We made a training plan based on the assessment of his logbook, crediting only those training entries that I was comfortable with. He completed our training and received a pilot certificate.

A few months later, Chase moved out of state and very soon after that, the FAA came knocking. An inspector from a far-away FSDO made a long journey to interview anyone and everyone at the flight school who had any contact whatsoever with Chase or his training. They declined to say why they were suddenly so interested.

The inspector had a stern face. He dismissed the normal pleasantries and got right to business. He had copies of Chase's logbook. He began asking about those entries, the ones from before. I couldn't talk about them. He was accusing. He continued to press hard for several hours, going over the same questions again and again. I had no information about training that occurred before Chase enrolled with us. The inspector became impatient and agitated. I wasn't responding to his interrogation the way he had expected. When he finally got to the part of Chase's training that we conducted and asked, "How did you...," I was glad to have my notes and the school's copy of Chase's training within easy reach.

I was able to show the notes from the initial logbook assessment and presented the reasoning for our training plan. We had documented how we ignored and didn't credit any logbook entry of a questionable nature. We had lesson plans with Chase's initials, verifying that he received our instruction. The inspector went line item by line item down the FARs, looking to see if we had overlooked anything. He voiced no complaints with what he found.

Our instructor assessments from his post-flight debriefings revealed that our training was obviously the first time Chase was exposed to maneuvers and information even though it had been recorded as previously covered. We gave Chase 40 hours of instruction. We filled in the blanks. We crossed the t's, dotted the i's, and polished him for what was a successful practical test.

The inspector wanted to keep our training record but I counter-offered with a copy. With his copy in hand, he was quickly gone. Whatever happened with Chase must have been big.

...

There are four important take-homes from this story:

First, in the *Aviation Instructor's Handbook*, buried deep in a paragraph concerning lesson plans, is a single mention of a pilot's training folder. Whereas the pilot logbook is the student's documentation of training, the training folder is normally the property of the flight instructor or school.

The training folder is where one can find copies of the student pilot certificate, lesson plans, quizzes, progress checks, the customer's preferred training plan, and a breakdown of the initial assessment and agreed-to costs to carry out that plan. Many of these items contain the pilot's initials. We filed copies of his airport-issued SIDA badge and a copy of his logbook. I had also filed a copy of the email I had written to request that someone at the FAA look into Chase. I prefer to keep copies of endorsements all together, on a separate piece of paper, in the training folder because these are the only items that instructors are required to keep for three years. I can discard the remainder at any time.

By far the most important items to keep are the instructor's notes. Well-documented, concise notes provide a basis for the instructor's rationale in adjustments to the training plan. Don't worry about making them super neat and tidy. Crumpled-up notes with coffee-ring stains show that it's a working file. It should show wear. It should be real.

It's important that an instructor keep evidence of training and discussions with a customer. It comes in handy should the time come to demonstrate your professionalism. The training record establishes written proof, before any controversy arises, that you provided quality instruction. Digital documentation is fine for tracking a student's progress. However, when it comes to professional documentation and protecting yourself from the accusation of errors or omissions, whether it be from a government agency or a civil suit, my lawyers have recommended paper and customer's initials. I never want to hear my lawyer say, "I told you so."

Second, the instructor who conducted training has the responsibility to record all training accurately, to write legibly, and to endorse it properly. Otherwise, this training cannot be credited as meeting the student's requirements for certification. In Chase's situation, our instructors repeated lessons because of the previous, unprofessional recordkeeping. This cost the customer time, hassle, frustration and money.

Third, an instructor looking to accept a student having previous training is responsible to verify that previous training is recorded accurately, is legible, and is endorsed properly. Otherwise, it must be repeated. In Chase's case, this is what kept our instructors out of trouble when the FAA started pounding for answers.

It can be very difficult to sit across the table and inform a prospective customer that you can't credit his flights. What I do is lay open the FARs. Point to the "solo requirements" and "solo cross-country requirements" and point to the paragraph that specifies "...must receive and log...." Then I direct the customer to find each required item in his logbook; if any items are not found, I start a list of those items that we must complete. Usually, in cases in which the list grows lengthy, I suggest the customer solicit the previous instructor to properly endorse the training he gave. I am happy to accept it if the previous instructor will do that.

When the customer begins to insist that training was completed, I acknowledge that it's only the paperwork in question. Still, the proper documentation is necessary. The customer may not like it, but he will view you as a careful, diligent instructor who follows the rules and records required training properly. It will be obvious that he should be angry and frustrated with the previous instructor rather than you.

Fourth, when dealing with this adversarial FSDO inspector, I strived to remain professional. I answered each of his questions fully, defending our position with facts—just clear, straight facts. When he pounded hard, I reminded myself that this wasn't about us. It wasn't personal; it was just business. He was doing a job. If I didn't know something or couldn't remember, I said that. Having good documentation made it easier. I referred often to the training folder. I may have bit my tongue a few times but in the end, I think he saw that I was truthful, consistent, and interested only in making Chase a qualified pilot.

We were lucky. In almost 50 years in the flight training business, no one was ever hurt flying. We never faced a lawsuit. However, when there were small incidents, the student training record was the first place the instructor would run. He wanted to make sure the record reflected well on him. Instructors all despised our record-keeping requirements, but they loved knowing it was there.

**Read more about these concepts in the** *Aviation Instructor's Handbook:*

Recordkeeping

# 6

stories
about

## planning
## instructional
## activity

Someone once told me that a good instructor would make a good pilot *even* while using a poorly designed syllabus. Alternately, a poor instructor will make a poor pilot *even* with a well thought-out, expertly designed syllabus.

Most CFI training focuses on developing a lesson plan with no thought to syllabus design. Yet for a CFI working at the average FBO, where every customer who comes through the door is as different as night and day, syllabus design or redesign is a daily task.

Like you, students are individuals with unique needs. No syllabus will meet every student situation. As an instructor, it's up to you to be flexible with syllabus redesign to meet those needs.

In this chapter, you'll meet a pilot requiring a checkout in an unfamiliar aircraft and another requiring a flight review. You wouldn't *think* these would be challenging customers or candidates requiring extensive planning for instructional activity...but you'd be wrong.

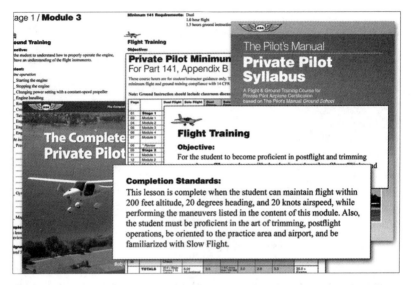

**Figure 6-1.** A curriculum and training syllabus provides guidelines which must be customized to meet the student's specific needs.

# Billy

He was a dentist but under his plain, white, lab coat beat the heart of an adventurer. Billy loved to travel. He ached to visit far-off places and meet interesting people. To him, general aviation was a tool to extend his three-day-weekend playground. Before Billy, I didn't understand the importance of adventure.

He passed a private pilot practical exam early in the week, having logged 50 hours. That same week, on Friday, he and his friends departed in a Cherokee 6 from KLEX to some exotic Caribbean island to SCUBA in deep blue waters.

Upon his return, I listened with great interest as Billy shared his many escapades. He'd flown over the Smoky Mountains and criss-crossed the ATL Class B airspace, with an abundance of ATC vectoring. After clearing customs, he arranged for an emergency raft and flew over waters dotted with cruise ships. He then filed an international flight plan, ventured outside the ADIZ, and landed in a foreign country. Once there, he purchased fuel in liters and paid for it in a strange currency. He had to pump it manually from rusty 50-gallon drums. He was satisfied, seeing it as a worthwhile journey. It intrigued me to think of his trip as real training that was also great fun. It inspired me to want the same type of experiences.

With Billy's encouragement, I began to include adventure in the flight training we gave at our flight school. The school's first "Adventure Flying Vacation" was a three-day weekend from Lexington to Key West. We put an instructor on board each plane and filled it with students. The trip departed in January. Our Kentucky pilots were more than ready to get out of the snow and into bathing suits.

For this adventure, we filled three planes. Students rotated seats at each fuel stop. Our students did the flying and logged the time. They landed on a tiny island airport with water on three sides. In the Keys, Billy offered a short SCUBA course to expose landlubbers to the ocean. He also arranged for us to experience sailing and deep-sea fishing. A few even participated in an old Key West tradition known as the Duval Crawl. We returned home for participants to arrive on time at work or school on Monday morning. The trip was a huge success.

Participants received *real* cross-country training and practical educational content. They met other pilots who enjoyed exploring and with whom they could share costs for future adventures. They operated advanced equipment not installed in normal training aircraft. They utilized basic stick-and-rudder skills in new ways. They built confidence in flying to new places and doing new things. Our students were out there doing what others were only reading about …and, they were having fun!

The Key West trip utilized every training opportunity. Based on where the student's training was in the syllabus, we arranged to fill needed aeronautical experience requirements. Those who required VOR navigation, nighttime, or flight by reference to instruments were assigned to fly an appropriate segment of the flight. We documented each student's training on a lesson plan once we returned home.

Soon instructors were planning to include an Adventure Vacation as part of their regular instructional activity. Instructors volunteered to plan and lead excursions to Oshkosh for AirVenture and to Lakeland for Sun 'n Fun. We flew to the Civil Aerospace Medical Institute (CAMI) in Oklahoma where students participated in high altitude physiology training. Students and instructors flew to Duluth to take delivery of a new Cirrus and to Wichita to pick up a factory-new Cessna 206. In both of these cases, everyone received factory tours and watched the assembly of airplanes. We also arranged journeys to sail in the Bahamas, snow ski in New Mexico, enjoy fall-foliage tours in New England, and a go on a Christmas shopping spree at the Mall of the Americas in Minneapolis.

Each jaunt had its unique learning opportunities. We built some purposely around the instrument long cross-country while others stayed with basic flying concepts. A few were better suited for high performance or complex airplanes. Training activities included day trips and weekend jaunts. Every journey provided opportunities for students to exercise aeronautical decision-making and risk management. They learned workload and task management.

The Alaskan Adventure was the largest, longest, most complex, most demanding, and most thrilling of our expeditions. Thirteen participants departed Lexington for a two-week adventure of a lifetime. Each student logged 50 of the most scenic and memorable hours you could imagine. Emergency equipment and survival gear became a large teaching opportunity. Each aircraft allocated 50 pounds for emergency gear. Each plane was required to carry a firearm large enough to put down a bear. Participants learned to shoot accurately and to handle a firearm safely as part of the knowledge needed to participate in this flight. How's that for incidental learning?

Over Watson Lake, about mile marker 635 along the ALCAN Highway, one plane experienced an alternator failure. Because our SOP required that the fleet travel together, all planes sat down for repairs. The City of Watson Lake in the Yukon Territory, Canada, was a tiny borough in the middle of nowhere and lacked any modern-day entertainment options. Nevertheless, asking a group of pilots to spend the day at the Watson Lake Airport Flight Service Station was akin to begging a child to play at Disneyworld. The students sucked on helium and laughed like Daffy Duck. They assisted in repairing weather collection equipment and learned, first-hand, the goings-on of a busy FSS.

Before all of that, however, about a month or so before departure on any adventure, students and the trip leader met to assess what specific knowledge each might need to make the flight most productive for them. With a study list in hand and knowing the deadline, students were motivated to ramp up their ground school. It did not require much to convince students to pass their FAA knowledge exam before an adventure. The prospect of having fun on such a trip was enough.

During preflight planning meetings, students would preview the route, discussing weather trends and terrain unique to the area. Small groups divided into teams for assignments. One team was in charge of controlling weight-and-balance while another would arrange ground transfers or supervise refueling at airports en route. Planning meetings were high-energy, stimulating learning experiences where students learned to gather information and make decisions. Our pilots-to-be were not spectators.

Our school saw a marked increase in the percentage of student pilots who completed certification as well as a decrease in time to certification. Students were training more frequently and for longer periods. They were passing the FAA knowledge exam earlier than the syllabus dictated and with higher scores.

Albeit extreme, our Adventure Vacations were one brand of scenario-based training. Billy taught me how to employ scenario-based training before it became trendy. He and I still share many flying adventures, including participation in The Flying Dentists Association. Many professional groups have an organization blending flying, networking and required continuing education.

...

The takeaway from this story is in plumping up *fun*. No student wants to be corralled into some practice area. Why not make the whole world a practice area? No instructor wants to be stuck in some traffic pattern. Why not use the traffic patterns of the nearly 13,000 general-aviation airports? Flight training should not be mundane!

Once an instructor has chosen a training syllabus and has gotten comfortable with the execution of each lesson plan, then it's time to venture away from the routine, to bring in flights having a mission—even if the mission is *just* to have fun!

Plan flights with a purpose. I found it helpful to start with a simple flight for a $100 hamburger. Then, as you become more comfortable in supervising students in more complex training environments, keep adding to the destination possibilities. You can sell education, safety and fun!

**Read more about these concepts in the *Aviation Instructor's Handbook:***

Training syllabus

Scenario-based training

# Lamar

Lamar owned several businesses spread across the southeastern states. His offices were located in out-of-the-way, sleepy towns connected by curvy two-lane roads. He racked up miles and wore out vehicles, driving cross-country to supervise his people. January through March was his busy season and family rarely saw him. If there was anyone who needed general aviation to simplify his life, it was Lamar. He earned a private pilot certificate and an instrument rating over the summer and accumulated 150 hours. Early that fall, he purchased a gently used but very sharp-looking Piper Lance.

In one fell swoop, Lamar jumped from renting a C172 to owning a 300 HP, turbo-charged, high-performance, complex, six-place, low-wing, T-tail. The Lance's service ceiling was 20,000 feet. It weighed twice as much as the C172. He was excited but also overwhelmed and intimidated by his new plane. He began to think that he had bitten off more than he could chew. He had, but we'd work through it, together.

We worked together to customize an aircraft-checkout syllabus having a logical series of training blocks and lesson plans so Lamar could eat this elephant one bite at a time. Dividing a big job into small pieces allowed him to feel accomplishment and it gave us natural points to provide feedback towards his ultimate goal.

The first block of training reviewed the aircraft POH and aircraft systems. It also included flying VFR maneuvers, along with constant-speed prop operations and takeoffs.

For a pilot transitioning into his first high-performance airplane, the emphasis is on learning the takeoff. The instructor must ensure that the pilot develops centerline discipline—that is, for the pilot to do what is needed to stick the nose wheel on the centerline and keep it there throughout the takeoff roll. The additional horsepower and its associated left-turning tendencies means the pilot must learn to be quick but gentle, with light pressure on the rudder pedals. Lamar had transitioned from 160 HP to 300 HP, requiring a lot of adjustment.

Lamar liked to wear leather cowboy boots with a chunky one-inch heel. Unfortunately, during our initial ground maneuvering in the Lance, the boots did not allow Lamar to feel the foot control he needed. We taxied back to the ramp where he changed into a pair of tennis shoes from his gym bag. I saw immediate improvement and he was happy about "feeling his feet" on the rudders.

After a little more practice in ground maneuvering, we headed out to the runway. We agreed that if the nose tire left the centerline, the takeoff was not successful. Lamar learned to take his time applying power for takeoff. He would first advance just enough throttle to get the momentum started. The heavy airplane required exaggerated rudder inputs compared to the C172. After he got his feet under him, he applied about half throttle. The second power adjustment was enough to cause her to veer hard left, but he was ready and reacted properly. Then at takeoff throttle, the rudders were astonishingly reactive and required only a big toe's pressure. He had to refrain from advancing to full throttle, as was done on the C172, to prevent the turbocharger from over boosting.

This training-takeoff profile took longer to develop liftoff speed. It caused the plane to remain on the ground for a longer period, but that was acceptable at this point in his schooling. We had a 7,000-foot runway. This method allowed him time to change his aircraft control priorities at the different stages during the takeoff roll. It also gave him time to think and to gain confidence in controlling his unfamiliar, oversized airplane. I didn't want him to be afraid of her.

After several takeoffs, he was soon able to handle a more normal, smooth acceleration. He was happy with the 1-1000, 2-1000, 3-1000 count from idle-throttle position to takeoff throttle. The nose wheel stuck to the centerline. He was ready to advance to Block Two.

For a pilot transitioning into his first T-tail, the instructor must ensure the pilot understands the aerodynamics involved. Slow flight, minimum controllable airspeed (MCA), stalls, takeoffs and landings are key so that the pilot develops a feel for the effectiveness of the elevator (or lack thereof) at slower speeds. Lamar and I did a lot of MCA practice so he would become proficient in airspeed changes and the control inputs required.

Next, we focused on landings and go-arounds.

For a pilot transitioning into his first complex airplane, the emphasis is on landing. The instructor must ensure that the pilot develops a standard operating procedure for pre-landing checklist and gear extension; that is, the pilot must establish a traffic pattern procedure and do it the same way every time. There's an old saying about pilots who fly retractable gear airplanes: "There are those who have and those who will," meaning that eventually a pilot will forget to put the gear down. Being faithful to a SOP is the pilot's best guard for not ruining a good day… or a good airplane.

Again, we established a profile involving tasks for each traffic pattern leg, designed to have the plane slowed and stabilized in the landing configuration early:

- *Downwind:* throttle reduced, slow to $V_{LE}$, gear down, check 3-green. First notch of flaps. Complete pre-landing checklist. Solicit an ATC clearance at mid-field. Second-notch of flaps and slow to approach speed before turning base.

- *Base:* GUMPS check. Verify 3-green lights, small power reductions for a glidepath to touchdown on the first one-third of the runway.

- *Final:* small power reductions to control glidepath. When runway is assured, add final notch of flaps and a GUMPS check. Crossing the threshold: again, verify 3-green.

- *After landing:* don't touch anything until the airplane is clear of the runway and comes to a complete stop.

This block of training required a lot of traffic pattern work. We used several local airports to broaden Lamar's perspective and to add variety and enjoyment. After several landings, Lamar was like a machine, consistently performing a smooth cockpit flow of his procedures. His SOP allowed him to slow his speedy plane, giving him the time needed to manage tasks and to stay in control.

Block Three featured emergency checklists, an emergency evacuation drill, and a gross-weight checkout.

For a pilot transitioning into his first six-place airplane, the instructor must ensure that the pilot learns to give a passenger briefing that is beneficial to five passengers. The pilot must also experience the handling characteristics of the plane at gross weight.

With only Lamar and me in the aircraft, we needed to add two cases of oil in the rear baggage compartment. Otherwise, the plane was nose heavy, which is not a good scenario for a T-tail aircraft. However, at max gross weight everything was different.

For today's flight, Lamar had invited four close friends to join his lesson. The first portion of the lesson was an emergency evacuation. The oil came out and friends climbed in.

I took a stopwatch and stood outside the plane. We agreed that for a successful emergency evacuation, everyone should exit the plane and meet behind the tail within 30 seconds. Everyone got in, belted up, and locked the doors. With no special instructions from me, Lamar gave his normal passenger briefing. On my signal, the stopwatch started. It looked like a Chinese fire drill with long-legged men tripping over each other's feet trying to get out. They were so determined I feared someone might get hurt. Their first evacuation time was one minute, forty-five seconds. *Not good enough.*

Lamar saw the tweaks needed to improve his passenger briefing. Soon he learned the words to say that communicated to everyone how they should get out of the plane. After four evacuations, everyone was out within our thirty-second mark. We can talk about passenger briefings all day, but nothing hits home like a pilot actually seeing his buddies tripping over themselves to empty a (simulated) burning airplane.

This is an example of good scenario-based training.

After all that aerobic exercise, everyone was delighted to go for a relaxing airplane ride. I was careful in the words I spoke over the intercom with Lamar's friends all able to listen, but I didn't hold back on high praise. We departed the home airport, flew to a local airport about ten miles away, and landed. Everyone got out for a quick break before the return flight home. I wanted two complete, separate flights. The added experience of putting passengers in the plane and dealing with the larger group was good practice. Lamar was astonished to find how different the plane handled in flight, having a full load on board.

He was very proud that his friends were able to see him solve problems and hear the compliments bestowed upon him. He had reached the pinnacle of Maslow's hierarchy of needs!

Block Four featured the POH equipment supplements and cross-country planning. It included an IFR, night, cross-country flight in the flight levels. Night doesn't add much to an IFR cross-country, but it allowed Lamar the opportunity to know his lighting system and the aircraft blind spots after dark.

For a pilot transitioning into his first turbo-charged airplane, the instructor must ensure that the pilot learns to be comfortable flying at higher altitudes with an emphasis on descent planning. We scheduled a ground session to introduce him to high-altitude operations and FARs before using performance charts to plan the flight. He developed a few simple math-truisms. For instance, if he kept his descent rate at 500 fpm, the amount of time needed to descend was double his change of altitude and 180 knots is roughly 3 miles per minute. As an example, if he had an altitude change of 8,000 feet, it would require 16 minutes and he would require 48 miles to make that descent. This made it easy for him to calculate mentally where to begin a descent from the higher altitudes.

Before our flight, Lamar had sported a trimmed goatee. Once he became familiar with the oxygen system and saw how the facemask fit, he knew his facial hair would prevent a good seal. I wasn't very surprised to see a freshly shaved Lamar. He was excited to get high and breathe some $O_2$!

The last block of training included all the IFR procedures. We even managed to work in a little actual cloud time. However, he decided his training would not be complete until he "soloed."

After his three solo takeoffs and landings, we cut his shirt and took photos for his Facebook page. I signed a high-performance endorsement, a complex endorsement, an Instrument Proficiency Check and an endorsement for WINGS—which reset his flight-review due date. Lamar's checkout required about 15 hours dual plus 12 hours of ground schooling, spread over three weeks. I'm sure he probably spent an additional 20–25 hours at home studying the aircraft POH and equipment supplements, calculating weight-and-balance, and flight planning. We were thorough in all aspects of his training.

I helped Lamar to schedule one of his first after-graduation trips to the chamber for high altitude physiology training. I wanted to set the stage for his continued training in the plane. We also scheduled a follow-up appointment after 90 days to verify that everything was going well for him. I wanted him to feel that our working relationship meant I was still there for him, for support and questions. Lamar logged over 500 hours the first year owning his new Lance and later upgraded to a Piper Malibu. Wanna guess who gave him that training?

...

It's common for an overzealous pilot to overbuy when purchasing an airplane. A wise instructor is vigilant about syllabus design. He allows the pilot to enjoy a wide variety of experiences in becoming familiar with his new purchase. The trainer thoroughly develops the pilot's basic stick-and-rudder skills in flying the unfamiliar plane. Otherwise, the pilot may never become completely comfortable flying her. That means he won't fully enjoy the ownership experience and he won't fly as often.

A carefully thought-out, customized training syllabus is the only way to achieve this. Lamar was a very proficient and current pilot. His training emphasized the differences between the airplane, the equipment and the SOPs with which he was already familiar, versus those on his Lance. We even revised his personal minimums, temporarily, until he gained additional experience in his new plane.

**Read more about these concepts in the *Aviation Instructor's Handbook*:**

Syllabus

Blocks of training

Lesson plans

Scenario-based training

Standard operating procedures

Maslow's hierarchy of needs

Pilot Proficiency Award Program (WINGS)

# Fred

At one time Fred had been a pilot of stature. He'd accumulated 1,000 hours and routinely flew IFR in complex airplanes. He loved travelling. He had visited most major points east of the Rockies via general aviation. He'd often bop up to New York to attend the release of a popular play or to Daytona to play on the beach for the weekend. Through the years, however, a divorce, a new wife and changes in life priorities diverted him away from flying. He had not been in an airplane in the past 25 years.

Fred plunked down in the lobby easy chair to inquire about "getting back into flying." He wanted to know what was required and how much it would cost.

What was "required" was a flight review consisting of two hours with me, including an hour in the plane. The cost was not too bad. However, I stressed that this was not his case. I went on to explain how the requirement assumed a current pilot and because of his long layoff, he'd require more than the minimum training. He grew impatient with my attempts at a full explanation. "Cut to the chase. I don't care about all that. Just tell me what I have to do and how much."

I shot from the hip: "25 hours on the plane and 50 hours with me." The cost was almost hurtful.

"Whoa!" He seemed taken back. "How did we get from one hour to 25?" Now he was interested in details. I was honest. I didn't have a clue about how many hours Fred would need. Between the voluminous changes in aviation over the past two and a half decades and having no idea what level of training he had previously or how much he had retained, it was impossible to give an accurate estimate. I based my guess on roughly one hour of refresher training for each year he'd been away. It was a starting point for budgeting purposes that I promised to hone after our first flight.

Fred required a customized training syllabus. His training had to touch on every aspect of VFR and IFR ground and flight to assure that his knowledge, skill, and SOPs were up-to-date with current industry measures. It was a big job. We agreed he would rent a Piper Arrow, an airplane he had flown often. At least we didn't have to throw an unfamiliar airplane into the mix. Fred and I worked together to build thoughtful lesson plans and packed each with review opportunities.

The bulk of Fred's training needs were in ground review. Much had changed since he'd last flown. He purchased a complete, online, ground-school package for private and instrument. It was more cost-effective than paying me by the hour to review with him. Additionally, it was more convenient for him to study when he had the time to concentrate. He promised to permanently store away his old training manuals. I feared the possible obsolete material they might contain. A new library of FAA handbooks soon arrived for him.

Fred was a dedicated student but we agreed to meet each week to assess his progress. He had a great number of questions as he tried to correlate how recent changes affected today's pilot. In training Fred, the only challenge was that I had to hear, over-and-over again, how his first instructor had done it. Fred had an endless stream of colloquialisms taught by his first instructor. At times, I wanted to find that first instructor to see what he was *really* like—no one could be that good.

A few items that had changed and needed additional discussion included plastic pilot certificates, English proficiency, and changes in medical certificate validity. He no longer needed an FCC Airman Radio License. Additionally, logging PIC hours, instrument currency, and the requirement to carry a photo ID had all changed.

We found the entire airspace system had changed during his absence, as had line-up-and-wait and taxiing clearances.

I introduced him to SIDA and airport security, DUATs, and a slew of online resources designed to help him. He needed to learn from scratch everything about the GPS system, GPS IAPs, using the iPad in the cockpit, and how to use flight-planning software.

Some of Fred's knowledge deficiencies were only nominally important but others were significant. At first I was inclined to use the PTS/ACS document as an outline for such a rusty pilot; however, doing so would have missed opportunities for us to discuss and un-learn obsolete material. His inquiries often included why the industry needed this new procedure or that regulatory change. He was interested to know what improvements the industry saw because of the changes. This often led into discussion about aviation accidents and significant industry events he had missed during his absence.

We agreed to an integrated flight-training approach, starting with VFR maneuvers, takeoffs, and landings and then moving into instrument procedures. Because he was an experienced pilot, he was able to communicate what he needed and wanted from me. Once his basic stick-and-rudder skills were up to par, he was quickly bored with the local routine. Fred wanted to go somewhere—like he used to. He didn't care about the process; he wanted to enjoy flying. He was anxious to revisit the practical skills he would be using while traveling with his family via general aviation. So, that's what we did.

One cross-country included his wife and teenage daughter on a trip to his beachside condo. He wanted to show them how useful this flying-thing could be for the whole family. Our cruise altitude put us right in the sweet spot, where we were continuously in and out of water vapor. Fred logged plenty of Direct-To GPS in IMC while refreshing IFR enroute procedures. He shot the IAP less than an hour before fog rolled in and closed the airport. He negotiated with the FBO for overnight parking, fuel, and a rental car. He was having the complete experience.

Fred's wife was happy that the whole trip was less than the time required on the airlines. It also excited her to see Fred in the role of pilot-in-command, and he was enthusiastic about sharing his love of flying with his family. Don't underestimate the importance of including the whole family in a student's flight training.

Another flight involved taking Fred's son to a baseball game. His son's weight was significant and the three of us were over max gross weight with full fuel, so Fred had the experience of draining 100-octane. This flight included a *real* short-field landing and a short-field takeoff after dark. It was VFR, but it was a black night without moon or stars. When there was quiet time en route, I quizzed Fred about something relevant, forcing him to think while flying.

Throughout his training, Fred documented everything with photos on his social media accounts. He loved keeping his friends updated on his path back to flying. However, before declaring Fred "finished," we agreed that he'd benefit from reliving a "solo" experience. Up he went for three takeoffs and landings. We celebrated afterwards with more photos and a dinner with the whole family.

I had to listen carefully to Fred. As a returning pilot, he thought he knew best what he needed. He had very strong opinions and he expected to have a say on everything we did. Within reason, I used a team approach in making decisions, structuring training goals and lesson plans.

Throughout Fred's training process, he constantly compared me to his previous instructor. I later learned this is perfectly normal. If the pilot loves flying, it's a good bet that his previous instructor instilled that love. The pilot will always appreciate that gift, but another instructor can rarely give it again. I have learned to accept it and not to take it personally. However, I didn't buy into the notion that this previous instructor was the saint Fred described him to be. It was only Fred's memory. Nevertheless, it is important not to disparage these memories.

A returning pilot needs the freedom to make mistakes, just like a student. At the same time, Fred did not like the title of "student" and didn't appreciate me treating him like one. Instead of saying something like, "you should know that, it hasn't changed," I used statements such as, "What works for me is..." and "I like to show pilots that...." I could see our old friend Maslow and recognized Fred's need for ego, belonging, and self-actualization. To him, this felt more as if we were colleagues comparing notes.

> **Read more about these concepts in the** *Aviation Instructor's Handbook:*
>
> Syllabus
>
> Blocks of training
>
> Lesson plans
>
> Scenario-based training
>
> Standard operating procedures
>
> Maslow's hierarchy of needs
>
> Computer-assisted training
>
> Integrated flight training

Fred returned to aviation because he remembered the fun. He recalled the joy that flying brought with it. He reminisced about how his life as a pilot was full of adventure. My training methods were acceptable only after I instilled that fun during his route back.

...

Assisting a rusty pilot back into aviation after a long layoff can be a daunting job for an instructor. An organized system of lesson plans ensures that details won't fall between the cracks. However, it also involves acknowledging the pilot's previous flight experience.

# COM/CFI

I'm not sure whose idea it was. It was the type that develops when somebody says something and someone else adds to it, and then a third person chimes in.

Before long, I had to leap off the chair and grab a marker to scribble thoughts on the whiteboard. It was a rainy day and a bunch of us flight instructors were sitting around the lobby bouncing around ideas on how to make our training more distinctive. As we talked, a new concept started to gel.

You've seen the syllabus that combines the instrument and commercial. Well, that never made sense to me. The material in those courses has absolutely nothing in common. The combined syllabus was designed for veterans using V.A. Educational Benefits because of a rule requiring vocational training. For the rest of us, combining these courses doesn't save any frustration or finances.

On the other hand, a combined commercial and flight instructor syllabus could be an efficient use of time and money. In addition, for an industry facing yet another shortage of flight instructors, it might provide a fast track for those local, mature pilots who are not airline-bound. These pilots reported interest in sharing their passion and experience with others—but they were not interested in a long, drawn-out training program.

A syllabus that would combine commercial pilot training and flight instructor training seemed logical. The information on knowledge exams for the two courses is very close. The big difference is that a commercial candidate reviews material while a flight instructor candidate must learn to teach it. Why do the job twice? It's very efficient to review the material while learning to teach it.

Even in the flight portion, the maneuvers are nearly the same, except that during flight instructor training they are performed from the right seat. I also knew from experience that newly certificated flight instructors don't feel completely comfortable flying and teaching from the right seat. They would like more hours in the right seat—without having to pay for them. So, why not initially learn the commercial maneuvers from the right seat? I mean, really, how often does a commercial pilot perform these maneuvers left seat, in the course of doing a commercial pilot's job?

The staff continued to powwow to design a very special course for those instrument-rated customers who we knew desired both a commercial and a flight instructor certificate. The goals of the new course were to learn it and teach it, then fly it. Pass three knowledge exams. Pass a commercial practical test and then within a few days pass the flight instructor practical. One course would culminate in two certificates.

Each lesson required a complex aircraft—one that does not require the PIC to occupy the left seat. The instructor for the course must be authorized to train initial flight instructors and the examiner would need to authorize the commercial practical test with the applicant occupying the right seat. We called around. Although some examiners would not agree, many agreed to try it after we explained what we were doing.

The idea was born. We designed the whole course that afternoon and had our first guinea pig—I mean, candidate—the following week.

Actually, he was a dispatcher who worked part-time at the flight school. We showed him our idea and his possible savings and he agreed to the experiment.

The innovative Combined Commercial/Flight Instructor Syllabus is available to download from the ASA website.[1] It turned out to be a lovely course. We had customers travel from out of state to participate in the program that was available only at our school. We had a new, unique product that generated new clients.

...

Creative syllabus design doesn't always require a complete redesign. Maybe it just needs a little tweaking. I view commercially available syllabi like frozen pizza: a good starting point that I can improve with added cheese and an occasional anchovy. It's up to the instructor to add the little extras. As an example, complimenting a standard syllabus with a free online video that teaches the benefits of a stabilized approach can reinforce the concept without adding expense to the student.

A commercially designed syllabus includes the minimum requirements and while I appreciate knowing everything is in there, I have no desire to produce a minimum pilot. I feel a system of training should provide a recipe to achieve the best-trained, safest, most proficient pilot. It's up to the instructor to pump up the value-add. You can implement simple strategies such as making each landing after solo something other than a normal one to give students more practice in short- and soft-field techniques, or including more landings after dark, neither of which require additional flight time or money.

Even if the syllabus is efficient, the instructor needs to add the motivation. My SCUBA instructor enticed me to jump into frigid water by talking about the unusual sea life and beautiful coral that I'd be seeing on this dive. My snow-skiing instructor induced me to tackle a slope I was reluctant to try by reminding me that it was the shortest distance to the hot chocolate and potty. It's up to the instructor to wrap a list of boring maneuvers into a lesson that's interesting and stimulating.

Sadly, no syllabus teaches how to develop character, leadership, professionalism, or ethical values in making pilots. It's left to the instructor, his methodology and teaching style to achieve those ambitious objectives.

If you are the kind of person who likes to put your personal touch on what you do, then understanding the basics of syllabus design will allow

---

1  http://www.asa2fly.com/Combined-Commercial-Flight-Instructor-Syllabus-P2445.aspx

you to create or tweak a syllabus that is uniquely yours and craft pilots you are proud to graduate.

I share this story as an example of how to design a new syllabus, using pieces and parts from an old one. The result can be a new and distinctive product to attract new customers and new business to an instructor. With a little creativity, you can play with lesson plans like Lincoln Logs®, taking pieces apart and putting them back together, in a different way, to make something original and unique.

**Read more about these concepts in the *Aviation Instructor's Handbook:***

Syllabus

Lesson plans

# 7

stories
about

## responsibilities &
## professionalism

It's said that A-List talent hires A-List talent, while B-List talent hires C-List talent.

What that means is that people who are at the top of their game recognize other people who are at the top of *their* game. A-List-ers surround themselves with only the best people to learn from and to help them improve. Conversely, those who are not at the top of their game don't hire top people because they don't want someone around who will make them feel stupid or who will outshine them. So, B-List-ers tend to hire the less capable, making themselves look good.

As a C-List CFI, your life as an instructor will be less than satisfying. Your mission is to become an A-List instructor. In this way, you will attract A-List clients who appreciate you as a person (and as a professional) and who are willing to pay for your talents and mentorship.

What is your definition of an A-List Flight Instructor? FAA manuals provide only a definition of the *minimum* requirements in knowledge and flight proficiency to pass a practical test. Those of us in the flight training industry are therefore free to define for ourselves the ethics, values and characteristics required to work at the top.

Notice that my suggestions for an A-List CFI consist of ethics and values rather than knowledge and skill. That's because a paying customer assumes that any FAA-certificated instructor is equipped with a professional level of knowledge and skill.

In the stories that follow, you'll meet instructors with the wrong stuff as well as a few with awesome stuff. You'll meet customers who made choices about the type of person they wanted to hire as their mentor, and the instructors who earned their respect.

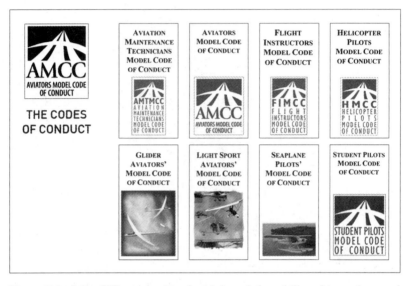

**Figure 7-1.** A-list CFIs are equipped with knowledge, skills, ethics, values, and professionalism. (www.secureav.com)

# Joe

It was obvious early on that he wasn't cut out for it. He may have had the right stuff, but not the right attitude. Joe was unhappy as a flight instructor.

In his defense, he had attended a very expensive flight school. He had decided not to work, but to concentrate on his studies in hopes of making the best possible grades. The result was that he was now drowning in a massive monthly student loan payment that a new flight instructor (or even a new doctor!) couldn't afford. His school had led him to believe that his take-home pay after graduation would be much more. In my opinion, he had not done his pre-school homework, choosing instead to trust in the marketing brochure and a convincing sales representative who offered a 100 percent student loan for tuition, books and living expenses.

Joe was anxious to fly for the airlines; after all, that's what he'd gone to school, studied, and worked for. He had done everything asked of him at school, but he was not flying for the airlines. He felt life was unfair. He felt stuck flying in a C172, and he felt it was unreasonable forcing him to instruct. It was unjust to expect him to build experience for a job he felt he already deserved.

Unfortunately for everyone around him, Joe brought this attitude to work. As his chief, I spoke with him about it. As much as I knew he needed the money, his paycheck continued to shrink as fewer and fewer customers chose to pay their money to endure his sour demeanor. He couldn't see that he was working against himself. The concept that he might need a second "dead-end job" to satisfy financial obligations was out of the question.

After a short time on the job, he began to complain about "instructor burnout," meaning that he was tired of instructing. He and I spoke about it. He didn't buy into the fact that there was, in fact, no such thing—it was only a poor attitude and a lack of professionalism. "You wanna talk about burnout?" I asked, "Think about the dentist who has to work all day bent over, peering into a stranger's mouth with bad breath and ugly teeth. You get to fly! You get to do (and get paid to do) what other people have to pay for!" He didn't buy in to the fact that to change his life, he had to change his attitude.

The final straw came the day I stopped at the coffee machine right outside the classroom. Joe was working with a customer. The customer was obviously having trouble. I overheard Joe say, "Come on, this is so simple! I've explained it before, why can't you get it?" *Ouch!* It rubbed me wrong that one of my good customers was belittled like that.

I added cream to my coffee and stirred. My ears still pricked up.

Joe continued, "If you're so stupid that you need me to do it for you, please just say so." *No, no, no!* This was not acceptable for any instructor to talk to a customer, in my book.

I added sugar to my coffee and stirred, interested to see what would come next.

Then I heard, "I'm telling you for the last time...." *Yes, you are!*

I picked up my well-stirred coffee, walked into the classroom, and in front of the customer informed Joe that indeed, he had just told *any* customer of mine "FOR THE LAST TIME." I added that he should clean out his locker and leave immediately. When Joe vacated the chair he'd been sitting in, I slid in, smiled at the customer, apologized for this distraction and offered a cup of coffee before continuing the customer's lesson.

An instructor's job is to help students learn. There is never, ever a case in which you would tell a paying client something *for the last time.* If you have to say it a hundred times, that's what you do. However, if a client must be told something repeatedly, I would suggest that maybe the problem is not the client, but the delivery method or teaching style of the instructor.

Look, I'm no angel. The daily grind takes its toll. We've all had bad days. We've all lost patience with a customer and said things we shouldn't. The difference is that a good instructor recognizes when his patience is pushed too far and takes a break before the crescendo. If the situation takes a downward turn, it might need an apology. If it was bad, a discount on the price of the lesson might be in order. The important thing is you admit what you did was wrong. You own it. You don't blame others.

It's the instructor's job to figure out how to reach that student. It requires an occasional step back to reevaluate what's working and to find a different way, if necessary. The student is an individual, just as you are. One student may need you to explain it, the next might need you to draw it, and still another might need to go out to the airplane and remove the cowling to touch it. Whatever you are doing, if it's not working, stop and approach it in a different way.

First, a flight school is a business. A business owner has to protect the investment in generating and keeping happy clients or the business will not survive. Professionalism doesn't have a practical test standard, it has a *customer opinion standard.* When it came to the customer, I had to demonstrate clearly that I recognized the problem and I was dealing with it cleanly, quickly, and for the customer's benefit. Otherwise, the business might lose a customer. Clients expect their time and energy to be well spent.

> **Read more about these concepts in the *Aviation Instructor's Handbook:***
>
> Aviation instructor responsibilities
>
> Professionalism

# Chris

I've trained, hired, supervised, and/or mentored hundreds of flight instructors over the course of three decades. The one that stands apart from all others in my memory is Chris. He wasn't the best pilot or even the best flight instructor. What stood him apart was that he knew how to be valuable to those around him.

Chris came to us still in his early twenties. His resume was already full of work experience, ranging from delivering newspapers to flipping hamburgers to harvesting tobacco. Part-time jobs, odd jobs, seasonal jobs—it appeared he appreciated a job and knew how to work. College had taken him six years, but he'd paid his own way and graduated with his education paid-in-full. I already respected the man for his work ethic.

Chris enjoyed living rent-free. He had built "a tiny house." He designed it with the help of a friend and they did all the carpentry, electrical, and plumbing. He showed it to me on his YouTube channel. It was a self-sufficient, well-appointed, man-cave built on a 12-foot flatbed. It featured a loft bedroom, heat, composting toilet, and rainwater collection as well as a solar panel to recharge the battery that powered his TV, kitchen appliances, and other necessities. With a quick hook-up to his truck, he was free to reposition his tiny home at a moment's notice for a weekend camping trip in the mountains or near a cool lake in the hot summer. Chris moved his tiny house from Iowa to Kentucky to work with us.

He had graduated college in December and started working for me in March. At that time of year, we were still experiencing overnight temperatures below freezing. Early mornings at the flight school often fell behind schedule. Getting the fleet ready to fly meant charging batteries, preheating engines, and removing frost. One day Chris walked into my office. "Chief, my schedule is not all that full yet. Would it be worth it to you to pay me a little extra to come in at o-dark-thirty to start turning icebergs into flying machines so that the instructors with clients don't fall behind?" Yes it was.

As spring progressed, our problems turned buggy. In Kentucky, it's a full-time job cleaning dead bugs from the airplane windshields once the weather turns warm. Chris was first up with an offer to do the job that everyone else hated. We continued him on a small base salary to compensate him for about 10 hours a week for his many talents, which he put to good use when not flying.

The following week I walked into the bookkeeper's office and noticed a significant change in lighting. "Wow! What's up in here?" I asked. The bookkeeper was thrilled. She had been complaining about dull lighting when Chris suggested they make a run to Home Depot for a new light fixture, which he quickly installed.

One day I passed Chris, hunched over, unclogging a sink. Soon after, he was standing on a ladder, removing the blinds from our floor-to-ceiling lobby windows so that the dispatcher could clean. He seemed to be everywhere, always doing something productive.

Chris was with a client when I noticed him start a clock-timer as they sat down to brief. I asked him about it later. He reported spending eight or nine hours at the airport and only getting paid for half that time. He was spending time with clients but found it difficult to charge them for it.

He decided to start a new habit of socializing with clients in the lobby for a few minutes at the start of their appointment. Then, when they were ready to begin work, they moved into the classroom, where he started his timer. The timer sat on the table all through the flight and until the conclusion of the debriefing. It helped Chris to stay on schedule and manage the customer's time. During invoicing, the timer revealed how much of Chris's time the customer would pay for. Chris was glad to be paid for all his time spent working and the client was comfortable that he wasn't paying for Chris's time while joking around and visiting.

When I checked the billing numbers, it was apparent that Chris's paychecks were higher than other instructors were, even though they had more students. The number of hours that Chris billed was significantly higher. It was 1999 and Chris was earning more than $35,000. I talked to his clients. They thought it was a fair system and were happy with it. I purchased a time clock for the classroom and Chris taught the other instructors his method. Everyone was soon on board and the time clock remained long after Chris had moved on.

By May, the school was operating at Mach speed and everyone was busy. I opened a kitchen cabinet door one day to find a stack of canned ravioli, soup, and packages of ramen noodles. Attached to the back of the door was a price sheet. "What's this?" I inquired. It was Chris's idea to stock canned food for those times when the instructors didn't have time to run out for fast food. He spent his money and time to keep it stocked. He collected money from sales and with the prices I saw, made a tidy profit for his troubles. On his last day, he negotiated for a younger instructor to purchase his inventory and to keep his "store" operating.

Hardly a week went by that Chris didn't identify a concern and attempt a solution. Not all of his ideas were great. Not all of his fixes were successful, but a few changed the axis on which my world rotated. He had become indispensable as an employee.

One day, Chris brought me a paper with notes on it. He had drawn an outline for normal radio procedures at our airport, step-by-step, with what the controller would say and how the student should expect to respond. "Chief," he said, "I do this same briefing with every student. Why don't we make a training aid as a tool to assist students in talking on the radio for the first few hours?" We did that and many other training aids, aimed at making it easier for students to learn.

Weekends were always a problem at the flight school. That was the time when most professionals and business clients were available for training. It was also the time when bright, young flight instructors wanted to socialize away from work. Chris decided that he'd like to work six days and then follow them with two days off. This meant that each week his days off fell on different days of the week. One week he was off Friday and Saturday, the next it was Saturday and Sunday, then Sunday and Monday, and so on. Soon all the instructors wanted to try it and we found that by staggering which days each instructor was off, the school was always staffed on weekends and yet every instructor had rotating weekend days off. His system lived on.

Most instructors are willing to do something when asked, but Chris was proactive. He had the ability to see what we needed. He built on the work of those who had come before him and left a legacy of his own. He improved the lives of his fellow instructors and made us, as a school, more valuable to our customers.

Students aren't equipped to assess what makes an instructor good, but most—the managers, professionals and business owners—can recognize a good employee. It feels familiar to them. They will assume that if you are a good employee, you are also a good instructor.

Offering to be helpful and performing menial tasks doesn't make you a lowly person. It marks you as a valuable employee: one who is willing to look after the small details so the customer's training is completed without interruption or distraction. As Chris used to say, "People of value, value people of value."

Chris was on staff for two years before Southwest Airlines scooped him up. I imagine his tiny home, parked atop some high mesa, silhouetted by a red sunset. Chris is probably inside planning the many ways he will one day revolutionize the aviation industry—and I expect he will.

**Read more about these concepts in the *Aviation Instructor's Handbook:***

Syllabus

Professional development

# Daniel

In 1959, Daniel was 18 years old. His dream was to become a rock star. He'd travelled to every back-road, redneck beer joint to play guitar with a band. In a short time, he'd become angry at the world that his big break had not yet come. He already felt older than his years. His great expectations seemed too far to reach. He didn't like himself.

One night, far away from home, in a drunken stupor, at a rowdy party with people who were not his friends, he killed a guy. The newspaper article that I found online included gruesome details. It had been a brutal murder. The jury deliberated for only 30 minutes. The judge gave him life in prison and despite his Kentucky roots, he served his time in the Colorado State Penitentiary.

Daniel had been a man-boy. He had assumed he'd receive the same respect his father had earned. He expected the comfortable lifestyle that his father worked for years to achieve. He was not patient for success. He didn't know how to work for it and because it didn't come fast enough, he'd grown sullen and bitter. He didn't appreciate what he had.

Daniel came from a hardworking family. His father was a simple salt-of-the-earth man. His mother had borne and raised twelve children. Through the years, as surrounding farmers sold off land, Daniel's parents somehow managed to buy it. Over time, they accumulated 9,500 acres. It was a working farm. All the kids worked on the farm and as they grew and married, their families lived together on the farm (if you can count spread across six counties as "together").

In 1999, after dozens of letters were written on his behalf, including the favorable recommendation of several influential statesmen, and at a time when prisons were overcrowded and low on funding, Colorado decided to parole Daniel and remand him back to the Bluegrass state. He would work at the farm in the family business. He would live under the watchful eyes of family and a parole officer. He had served 40 years in prison.

It was 2000 when Daniel stood before me, hoping for the highest form of freedom. He was a smart-looking man. Any woman seeing him on the street would look twice. His blue jeans fit snug around the thighs. His crisp white T-shirt hinted at a muscular chest and the blazer pleasantly hugged his biceps. He stood only five and a half feet but carried himself tall. Daniel was the picture of health with clear eyes and smooth skin. Despite his age, his hair was still full, thick and black. "Hello ma'am, I'm Dan'l." He spoke softly. Not at all what I had expected.

His parole officer had called the day before to set up the meeting. He was upfront about Daniel's story. He wanted to know if our school would be willing to teach Daniel to fly. As chief instructor it was my decision. "You're kidding, right?" was my shocked answer. The parole officer believed that Daniel had been a stupid kid who mixed up with the wrong crowd, and that in prison he had matured into a worthy man. He wanted Daniel to have his dream. Daniel had agreed to wear an ankle bracelet—one that would allow law enforcement to track him—in exchange for being able to take flight lessons. The family would foot the bill. It was actually because of the good-hearted, well-intending parole officer that I agreed to meet Daniel, but only that, just to meet.

My businesswoman head wanted to scream, "Hell no!" but my heart answered otherwise. He had paid for his crime. Perhaps flight training would reinforce his personal responsibility and accountability. Maybe finding accomplishments would build his ego and allow him to lead a normal life. Perhaps he would reveal a positive message for others.

I am by no means a bleeding heart for the downtrodden. Still, I could not slam this door closed for Daniel. It would be up to him to do the work if he were up to the challenge. Besides, I told myself, how much did I really know about the backgrounds of my clients? Statistically speaking, there must have been more than a few jailbirds to fly through and I just didn't know about them.

Then suddenly, the businesswoman reared her head again: what would other customers think? Did I have an obligation to brand him or to warn others? How would my staff feel? Should these people have a vote in whether to socialize with a felon or even if they wanted to sit next to him in an airplane? I decided the instructors should know. Otherwise, I jeopardized their trust.

It was a heated staff powwow. We debated all the questions one might expect under the circumstances. My management style is about effective decisions and successful operations. I didn't have answers but it was up to me to set the mood. We would approach Daniel as an individual. We would take things one day at a time. We would see what we saw and deal with it. Any instructor who so chose was not required to fly with Daniel, but they were required to treat him with the respect due any customer. If no instructor wanted to teach Daniel, I would do it.

I flew with Daniel on a small number of lessons but after that, another instructor stepped up to the job. Daniel proved to be docile and compliant. He never complained and never whined. He was joyful every minute he was in the air. His knowledge-test score demonstrated his diligence for studying. The staff came to respect his work ethic. In the end, I think most of the staff worked with him on some level or another. Over time, they were increasingly willing to consider him "an OK guy." Daniel passed the practical exam on the first attempt.

Daniel, to his credit, had somewhere learned to be patient with us. He did not hide from his past. He understood how people viewed him. He saw and appreciated that small successes along the way contributed to his ultimate goal.

He found ways to be useful around the flight school, helping with safety seminars, cooking at pancake breakfast fly-ins, and encouraging the newer students. He joked and played with everyone. He was the first to volunteer, helping anyone in need of assistance. He took every opportunity to appreciate vocally everything and everyone in his life, which in turn reminded us all to be appreciative of all that was good in *our* lives.

...

Being a felon, Daniel was not an obvious candidate to be a pilot. People with disabilities are another example of those who are not obvious contenders. Yet, over the years, we trained a paraplegic confined to a wheelchair; a pilot with a prosthetic leg; as well as a flight instructor who had only one arm. I met Jessica Cox once, the pilot with no arms who flies with her feet. Sometimes people who you don't, at first, consider for training are the most motivated to learn and the easiest to teach.

Having said that, a pilot candidate who is deaf, mute, or missing a limb requires special training. They aren't the best client for a newly certificated flight instructor. Don't be afraid to recommend a more experienced instructor or an organization such as the Deaf Pilot's Association. These organizations have uniquely trained flight instructors and use specialized training aids.

Because pilot candidates feel somewhat intimidated and vulnerable on their first visit to the airport, it's important to have a semi-private area available when speaking with prospective clients. I was happy to have a semi-private area when speaking with Daniel. It allowed me to ask openly that which was bearing heavily on me and it allowed him to be honest with his answers.

**Read more about these concepts in the *Aviation Instructor's Handbook:***

Helping students learn

For most potential clients, the subject of money is a sensitive matter. Other topics that some might consider private include medications,

Physiological obstacles for flight students

misdemeanor run-ins with the law, advanced age, previously failed exams, and their disenchantment with another flight-training provider. Some are nervous about being accepted for who they are. A confidential area will encourage them to be forthcoming with information that the instructor may require to serve their needs.

# Clay

I found Clay extremely pleasant and charismatic. Talking and laughing with him on the phone was easy. He was very excited about flying. He had owned a pressurized, multi-engine Navajo for three years and had logged about 400 hours in her. He used his plane most often to advance his successful real estate development company that had ongoing projects around the region. During our discussion, we found much in common and compared stories about flying into airports we had both visited in Florida and Colorado.

Clay's insurance company required the pilot to have annual training from a school approved by them. We were such a school. He scheduled training the following week. He planned to fly in each morning, train all day, and fly the 30 minutes to return home each night.

The Navajo taxied up to the flight school ramp, right on time. I watched from the lobby window as he took his time in shutting down the cockpit, stowing checklists, and installing control locks. Climbing out of the plane, he chocked all three wheels. My first impression was that of a meticulous and purposeful pilot. I already liked this guy.

In the classroom, the instructor reviewed with Clay the insurance-approved syllabus. Clay seemed excited about the prospect of completing a thorough and well-organized training program. He was excited to have detailed instruction and descriptions of his aircraft's systems. He enjoyed learning and considered himself a diligent student.

That's when the problems began. The instructor beckoned me, as chief, to the classroom for a powwow.

Clay was confused about the completion standards. He didn't understand how he could possibly complete an Instrument Proficiency Check when he was not an instrument-rated pilot. In fact, he had not yet passed a private pilot checkride. *What?!?*

His student pilot certificate was valid, complete with each proper endorsement. His logbook documented all the requirements had been met. His maneuvers, the pre-solo knowledge exam, and cross-county training in the Navajo were current and professionally recorded. Endorsements were clearly written for solo cross-country flights to several destinations in Florida and Colorado, as well as an endorsement for repeated solo cross-country to KLEX. Although unexpected, everything seemed to meet the letter of the FARs.

I was having trouble getting my head around this and needed to speak with Clay's instructor back home. As it turns out, Clay started training in a C172 but soon found the opportunity to purchase this Navajo at a basement price. The instructor was the seller's pilot and he would be losing his job when the Navajo sold. Clay purchased the Navajo and hired the pilot to manage one of Clay's enterprises in exchange for the instructor's agreement to fly and complete Clay's training in his new Navajo.

Through the years, after Clay learned the skills to do what he wanted and had the means to do it legally, he found less value in passing tests and achieving a certificate. At the same time, the instructor found it increasingly difficult to say "no" to such an amiable and pleasant boss, who was paying him generously at a job he really liked. The instructor idolized Clay but was very hopeful that our school could work out a plan for his certification.

*Well, now…this put a different slant on the training plan.*

Rule #1 in flight training: Don't make *any* assumptions about clients or their training needs. Clay did not intentionally deceive me. He simply told me stories of his flying experiences and I drew my own incorrect assumptions. That is why the first thing that we accomplish with every new client is a review of certificates, flight records, insurance requirements, and maintenance logs—with no assumptions about anything. Following this one simple rule has saved us hordes of embarrassment and uncomfortable discussions with FAA inspectors.

I agreed that our instructor would deliver ground training that day. In the meantime, I needed time to think about how we should handle our newest client.

Clay became so immersed in learning that he overstayed his intended departure time. By the time he gave thought to the flight home, the skies had grown dark. His instructor's authorization for cross-country specifically listed a no-flight-after-dark limitation, even though Clay had completed night training and the instructor had previously OK'd night flight. I inquired if Clay needed a motel room.

Clay expertly began his verbal maneuvering. Obviously, he was experienced in negotiating a deal. He was charming and gracious. He was insistent that it was legal; that he had done it safely many times before; that it was only a thirty-minute flight; and that I should endorse him for his flight, after dark. I could now see the problem from the perspective of his instructor back home, but I told Clay, "No."

In my opinion, Clay was a risky client. He wasn't a bad pilot or a bad person but his situation was not the industry standard. True, he'd flown his plane for hundreds of hours over several years, but eventually it had to catch up with him and the instructor who authorized it. In my opinion, his tolerance for risk was too high and he had a distorted view of what was safe for him. Although he was an eager learner, he was not willing to consider any recommendations we had for improving his safety.

He began tempting me with promises of opportunities for my newest instructor to accumulate multi-engine hours. If I wouldn't do it for him, wouldn't I do it for my staff? "No."

I'll admit that my moral compass quivered away from true north for a few moments. Clay's arguments were reasonable, logical, and legal. I began to think harder to find a win-win resolution. However, it bothered me that while he asked that I give way, he was steadfast in his requirements.

He had two sons who were also interested in flight training. There could be two additional students and future business for my school, if only I could help him get home with an endorsement. "No."

As a businesswoman, I evaluate opportunity, risk, and reward. With Clay, the opportunities, I told myself, could be great but the risk was staggering and the reward slim when I considered the amount of profit I could gain with Clay versus how much I would spend on attorneys after his accident.

He was polite but insistent. His instructor back home had done it, why wouldn't I sign my name in his logbook, right here? He even had an ink pen standing at the ready. "NO!!!"

Here is the concept that will stop any client from harassing you. Feel free to use similar words to stop any disagreement when a customer expects you to bend for them:

> "As an instructor, I have a set of rules that I follow. They have served me well. I like my rules. I don't break them for anyone because they are in **your** best interest—even if you can't see that right now. I respect that another instructor may use different rules. But if you choose to work with me, we use my rules to keep you safe."

Saying something similar signifies where your values are. It sends the message that you are concerned for the customer's well-being and it does so without being critical of another flight instructor.

Sometimes what a student asks for is legal but it's not the right thing. The FARs don't put a limit on how long someone can be a student pilot, nor do they place limits on how far a solo cross-country may be, or how many nights can be spent at the destination before returning home. Those burdens fall to the flight instructor as the expert most knowledgeable about the student, the plane, and the training environment. You may think it's appropriate to solo a student pilot, in a plane like a Navajo, from Kentucky to Colorado for a week, then endorse him appropriately and you'll both be legal—but that doesn't make it a smart thing to do.

With the FARs as your benchmark, you are using the lowest possible bar. I don't recommend the FARs as justification for your actions and opinions. If you do, then you will never teach clients to respect personal minimums. You lose the opportunity to highlight risk management and you lose the respect of a client—now they know that you don't have personal principles.

To give credit where it's due, Clay's instructor did a good job of keeping every endorsement current and his boss legal. He performed within the limits of the FARs. This brings me to talk about "professional courtesy." In my opinion, professional courtesy dictates that I never speak badly about another instructor. I will assume that I don't know all the details. I respect that they work under a different set of ethics and safety parameters. I can talk badly about the result of their work when I find it lacking but I am not disrespectful of the person.

In all fairness to Clay, he was careful to stay within the bounds of what was legal. He spent the night but cancelled the remainder of his training. Unfortunately, my refusal to endorse his night flight resulted in his discontinuing training with us. I didn't pursue him as a customer, feeling that our goals weren't aligned and that he wanted only an instructor he could manipulate into doing what he wanted.

**Read more about these concepts in the *Aviation Instructor's Handbook:***

Aviator's Model Code of Conduct

Personal minimums

Evaluation of student ability

# Cooper

Cooper was to be the fourth generation of pilots in a prestigious family rooted in the local area. He had an ivy-league education with several advanced degrees, including a PhD. He owned a successful business and used general aviation to get him close to his clients quickly. I felt honored that he chose me as his instructor.

At 28 years old, he was skinny and lanky. The most prominent feature on his face was his mouth and his favorite word to come out of that mouth was "f**k." Cooper is the only person I ever knew who would use the F-word as a verb, a noun, a pronoun, and an adjective. Many times, he favored multiple iterations in the same sentence.

It's not that my feminine sensibilities were offended when he dropped each F-bomb; I simply found it tedious to listen to him. Filtering through all that f-stuff to reach his underlying message was not an efficient way for an instructor and student to communicate. It was difficult to interpret his simplest question. I begged him multiple times to tone it down and explained why it was important to do so. Multiple times, I watched as my words drifted into one ear and out the other before evaporating into thin air. *Poof.*

It was, I think, about his fifth flight. We were 2,500 feet MSL, returning to the airport from a fun-filled lesson introducing ground-reference maneuvers. It was a blue-jeans-and-flannel-shirt kind of morning. The leaves on the trees below us were at peak fall color. Tower frequency was filled with chatter from multiple aircraft inbound for the big football game between the University of Louisville and University of Kentucky. Everyone seemed to enjoy the day. I was prepared to take over radio coms if needed but so far, Cooper was doing a great job. I caught his eye, flashed a big smile, and gave him a thumbs-up for reassurance.

The controller had asked him to report, "Traffic in sight." I had just cast my eyes in the direction I supposed traffic to be when suddenly in my headset, I heard Cooper's voice depart from standard pilot/controller terminology. He unleashed a barrage of F-expressions into my ears. It was one of those occasions having an F-noun, an F-adjective and an F-verb, and it seemed to go on forever. I reached to unplug his finger from the push-to-talk switch but it was too late. It was done. It never occurred to me that he would use his favorite F-word on the radio but looking back now, I guess I should have anticipated it.

All chatter ceased. The frequency was abruptly dead quiet. I held my breath and time stood still. The controller finally recovered from his shock and commanded, "Call the tower after you land." Cooper's eyebrows bounced up, "Am I f***ed? I mean, am I in f***ing trouble?"

"Nope," I exhaled, "I am."

The tower chief required a personal meeting. I set the appointment to be during my next scheduled time with Cooper. I hoped that having Cooper there would help him to learn the result of his F-inclinations. I pretty well knew what to expect with the tower chief and wanted Cooper to witness firsthand how his F-routine had reflected on both of us. He needed to be convinced that it wasn't just my personal opinion of his lexicon. He needed to know that some behaviors are simply unacceptable in our industry if he wanted to become a successful pilot. I reckoned the tower chief was about to help.

He did. The tower chief was surely a retired boot-camp drill sergeant. He didn't hold back. He unleashed everything at me and occasionally stood on his tiptoes to get up directly into Cooper's face, too. He was a man of very few but loud, descriptive words. He wasn't yelling but still, his voice thundered. The tower chief made it clear that "there *will* be respect for other people on the frequency, even if you don't respect yourself." He talked about the interruption to other air traffic and the disruption throughout the tower facility as controllers reeled from the aftereffects of what Cooper had said. The meeting took five minutes but it took a year off my life.

I was still shaking from the tower chief's reprimand. It was even more intense than I had foreseen. Cooper and I walked through the parking lot toward the car. In all heartfelt sincerity he hung his head and blurted, "Oh, f**k Arlynn, I'm so f***ing sorry."

Comfortable in my decision I announced, "Cooper, it would be best if you continued training at an airport without a tower facility."

"F***k no, not unless you will still f***ing work with me." He almost begged.

"No. You can't control yourself and I can't prevent you from doing it again. I can't trust you." I ended his training with me.

Over the next few weeks, I took multiple calls from Cooper. I liked him. When he offered that I could charge him money if I caught him using the F-word, I began to think that might just work and allowed myself to be persuaded. These were the conditions:

1. The F-habit had to stop, right now, immediately—if not sooner. I had no more patience. None. I was not going to risk *my* FAA certificates over this.

2. Cooper would not again talk on the radio until I was convinced that he was under control of his F-pattern. I could not trust him and could not risk another F-explosion.

3. Not having the normal practice communicating on the radio would delay his solo.

4. Knowing he was a businessman and that money was a large motivator, he was to be charged $20 each time that I heard an F-utterance. It didn't matter if he spoke it to me or to someone else in the room. It didn't matter if I overheard it during a phone conversation. If my ears pinged an F-phrase, I added it to his tally.

This was all that I could think of to motivate him to break his F-fondness. He agreed to all conditions. We resumed training. Our next appointment cost Cooper $200 for the flight lesson plus $300 for the newly created F-fund. I could see no apparent lessening in his F-thing. Perhaps he thought I was not serious but I was determined to break his F-addiction.

Cooper had other options. There were plenty of other instructors around, many with more experience and most, I presume, who would be less harsh. He never said it, but I believe he continued to train with me because he knew that I sincerely wanted him to be successful. I think at his core, he was ready for this change.

Over the months that followed, Cooper broadened his vocabulary, omitting the one word I had grown weary of hearing. On checkride day, I paid his examiner fee and aircraft rental. Later, we-plus-spouses celebrated graduation with a nice dinner at an upscale restaurant. I paid all the day's festivities with F-money.

Later that same year, Cooper returned for an instrument rating. He purchased an airplane and through the years has purchased several more. He was a graduate that I took pride in creating. He moved out of state but he continues to fly and to support his local general aviation community.

...

Turning out a successful pilot requires the instructor to influence certain habits. Some habits are more difficult to influence than others.

Establishing a new habit requires the instructor to be persistently insistent. However, as long as the student trusts that the instructor has his best interest in mind, he will usually—eventually—be responsive to change.

These days, the F-word is no longer considered crass in some circles. That happens. Societal morals fluctuate every few years. Today, words like "tolerance" and "social justice" are in vogue, leaving some instructors to believe that we should accept and dismiss certain behaviors. It doesn't matter how general society may lean. No matter what society teaches as the norm, our community—the aviation industry—has a strict set of rules, behaviors, and habits that are required for our success. The rules for safety seldom change.

Just like "transfer of learning," personal habits will, in time, transfer themselves into cockpit habits. The instructor is the gatekeeper. An instructor may have to introduce concepts like *self-sufficiency* to help promote single-pilot resourcefulness; *personal responsibility* to help promote risk management; and *accountability* to assure that FARs and the rules of good common sense are respected.

**Read more about these concepts in the *Aviation Instructor's Handbook:***

Syllabus

Ensuring student skill set

Evaluation of student ability

The instructor is responsible for the result of his or her overall finished pilot-product. It's worth the effort to produce a good aviation citizen because, in the end, we share the sky and the airport with our graduates.

# Howard

He was a shiny man. His shiny, black, patent leather shoes perfectly matched his belt. Jewelry sparkled from his neck and around both wrists. Diamond rings encircled several fingers on both hands and an oversized watch completed his attire. His pearly whites reminded me of a movie star and he had a full head of white hair that glistened under florescent lights. Howard shimmered from head to toe. I never did learn what he did for a living. His answers to my polite inquiries were vague and mumbled. After a while, I stopped asking. It became obvious he didn't wish to talk about himself.

Howard's PA46 Malibu had been in the maintenance shop for almost a year undergoing extensive repairs. He was not specific about what kind. I didn't know how long he'd owned the plane or how many hours he had logged in it. He didn't offer any information about himself. He did offer, however, that even though he had not flown during the time the plane was in maintenance, he felt "fine to fly." His insurance required annual recurrent training and it was only because of this that he'd come to our school.

The logbook I saw was labeled "#3." It had slightly more than 1,000 hours recorded "From Previous Page"—leaving me to assume that he'd filled books #1 and #2. There were only two entries in his latest log. It didn't tell much about his flying habits or his currency but it didn't matter; we'd bring him up-to-date with all new endorsements before releasing him into the skies.

His insurance-approved syllabus mandated three days of recurrent training. On his first day, he made it clear that he would not enjoy the training, nor was he happy with me. His "instructor back home" didn't expect him to recite regulations from memory. He felt it "unfair" to ask him to compute a weight-and-balance when his flying never included passengers. Moreover, there was "no reason" to calculate takeoff or landing distances when he only flew to airports having more than 5,000-foot runways. During our short recesses from training, he would constantly lean over the front desk counter, complaining to the dispatcher about how stupid this all was.

After lunch, we went flying. His preflight inspection included only checking the quantity of oil and fuel. He operated in his own little world without any kind of situational awareness. He had become accustomed to punching the autopilot to ON immediately after takeoff and turned it OFF immediately before landing. He was totally dependent on the moving map display for navigation. He sulked and complained about performing each maneuver. His hand-flown IAPs were all over the sky. His constant use of technology had degraded his basic skills terribly. It was a long first day for both of us.

When he didn't show up for his second day of training, it was almost a relief to everyone. Still, at 9:00 a.m., I called to inquire about his tardiness. "I'll tell you what the holdup is," he said, "You guys are a royal pain in the a$$! You are wasting my time. I don't need your kind of training. I am *not* coming back!" We were more than happy to refund the unused portion of his prepaid tuition.

It was about two weeks later when Howard called again. This time, his demeanor was markedly friendlier. He wanted to set up training for later that week. I assumed this was a continuation of his recurrent training and prepared accordingly. I was wrong.

Sitting across the table, he seemed smaller than in our previous time together; the shimmer was off. After the routine morning pleasantries, he settled into the leather chair and began to speak. As he relayed it, he'd flown about 10 hours since we'd last seen him. On his last flight, everything was fine—until it wasn't.

He had cancelled IFR to do a visual approach into his destination when, somehow (he didn't know how this happened) he accidentally flew back into the clouds. He then became disoriented—perhaps that avionics problem had not been properly repaired in the shop. Because he was disoriented, he called ATC for assistance. (That's what they're there for, right?) According to them (he didn't believe they were correct), he had busted the CVG Bravo Airspace. So there he was, in thick IMC, in the middle of Bravo Airspace, and without appropriate clearances.

Following that flight, there had been a brief phone call from the FSDO. A few days later, Howard's invitation for a 709 arrived in the mail. The "709" is short for CFR 44709, which is the regulation that gives the FAA the authority to reexamine a pilot. The FAA initiates a reexamination when evidence leads to questions about a pilot's qualifications. If the pilot is found deficient in skills or knowledge, the pilot certificate can be revoked. The FAA specifically directed Howard to return to our school in preparation for his 709.

The FAA doesn't want to revoke a pilot's certificate. If a pilot makes a mistake, the FAA wants to know how and why it occurred. What they really want is for the pilot to receive remedial training from a good provider. Training in preparation for a 709 is usually extensive because so much is at stake. Howard thought it was all very stupid to waste the government's time and money like this. After all, it was only a *small* slip up. He thought it silly to come to my school when there was an instructor right on his home field who should be able to do the training.

After hearing his story, I asked to see the FAA's letter ordering the 709. The letter stated that his privileges were suspended until the 709 was passed, which meant he could not fly as PIC. Yet, Howard had flown his Malibu from his home airport to KLEX for our meeting.

It appeared to me that Howard did not understand the seriousness of the situation. I explained that his certificates were on the line. He had to nail this checkride. I further explained that an instructor must accompany him home and be the pilot-in-command. Once again, he gave every appearance of being unhappy with me.

Now, with training focused on preparation for his 709, we pressed him even harder to know the FARs and to perform careful preflight preparations. I could see his body language hardening and the furrows forming above his eyebrows. I could see the veins on his neck pulsing with heightened blood pressure. The fingers on his hands resting on the tabletop had curled into tight fists. He hated being forced into training and even more, he hated being forced to train with us. He loathed every second until he could take no more. He finally blew a gasket, "I can't believe you guys are treating me like this! What sons of bitches you are! You're wasting my time. I'm out of here!" The Malibu flew away.

A couple of days later he flew, solo, into the airport to meet with the FAA inspector. An hour later, as I understand it, he rented a car to drive home with his certificates revoked.

...

As instructors, we should have a good reason for prescribing specific training to a client. We should be able to justify why we think training is required, important, or otherwise needed. In the perfect situation, we should manage a customer's expectations *before* training begins. It doesn't matter what the training is for—an initial certificate, a flight review, or an aircraft checkout—we should outline a specific training program with anticipated hours; an accurate and honest itemization of costs; and completion standards. The client should have the opportunity to negotiate in certain areas those things which they want included. Just like a hamburger, all should agree on the final product sold and purchased.

Howard's situation was not ideal from the beginning. He was not able to negotiate the content of his training. At first, it was his insurance company's requirements. Then later, it was the standard of the practical test that dictated the level of proficiency required to pass the 709. I understood Howard's frustration, but there was little that we as instructors could do about it. Our only option was to provide quality instruction.

I felt our first obligation was to the industry, to assure that every pilot we train is a safe one. Our second obligation was to the insurance company to deliver the approved syllabus, thus maintaining our insurance-approved-school status. Our third obligation was to Howard, to ensure he passed his 709.

As an instructor, you are selling more than an hour of aircraft rental and your time. You are promoting a skill set, wisdom, guidance, safety, and a total training experience. As long as you first approach training as a customer-service experience, then if you are faced with a similar situation—a client who doesn't appreciate you—then let them go. Fire your customer. Don't apologize. Simply smile and say, "I wish you well in your future aviation endeavors," and hold the door for them to leave.

It's not necessarily your fault, nor is it the client's fault that the relationship didn't work. Sometimes your first obligation is not to the customer. Sometimes, the problem may only be that the customer wants a Walmart product and you are delivering a Macy's product. Sometimes the customer is *not* always right.

**Read more about these concepts in the** *Aviation Instructor's Handbook:*

Professionalism

Providing adequate instruction

# Katie

Katie had completed initial flight instructor training elsewhere, but her practical exam, administered by the FAA, had not gone well—twice. In a desperate attempt to find the secret to passing, she'd asked the FAA inspector how she would ever pass. His response was, "I'd fire that flight instructor of yours. He's obviously not getting the job done."

She came to train at our school. It was February, and she hoped to be working as an instructor by spring when flight schools everywhere begin the mad dash to hire fresh faces. That gave us about six weeks.

Although Katie's training with us was not complete, she was back in my office to ask, "Would you look over my resume?" Her old school had given her a template. She'd used it and had already emailed a flurry of resumes. She didn't receive a single response from prospective employers. She sensed something was missing, and she was right.

Resumes of new flight instructors all have a similar look. Using a resume template with the same lackluster objective, "To obtain a flight position in the aviation industry," is guaranteed to put any flight school manager into slumber land. Katie later chose to trash the template and build a resume that stood apart from the others, to be unique and memorable. Before sending it out, however, she needed to plump up her professional credentials to elevate her resume to the top of the heap.

Katie removed garbage information—that is, anything that didn't document her as being at the top of her game, including knowledge exam scores. The same goes for pilot certificate numbers and medical status. People with no experience expand these items to take up space on the paper. One other point: By listing hers as a "FAA license," Katie had documented that she missed at least one important class!

According to the TSA, every instructor is required to have a Flight School Security Awareness Training Certificate, but some instructors don't do it during training. By completing this training and receiving a completion certificate, Katie demonstrated that she was work-ready for prospective employers. She added this training to her resume. The cost of this training was *free*.

Katie earned her CFI certificate and along with it her WINGS credits. Documenting her flight instructor training on the faasafety.gov website fulfilled most of the requirements to complete her WINGS. The one item she lacked was a free online course that required about an hour to finish. By becoming involved in the FAA Pilot Proficiency Award Program, Katie demonstrated her knowledge of the program and her support for this industry-wide aviation safety initiative. She added this to her resume. Her WINGS cost Katie nothing.

She became an FAA Safety Team Representative and she hosted a safety seminar. As a FAAST rep, she found many advanced resources to use in training students. In hosting a safety seminar, Katie met the pillars of the local aviation community. She also landed her first dual given, as one of the participants hired her to complete the flight portion of WINGS. She added her FAAST designation and the safety seminar to her resume. In addition, she now had two hours of dual given where she previously had none. She was thrilled to be paid for work!

Each spring, FSDOs across the country host recurrent training for designated pilot examiners. Flight instructors, even those in training, are encouraged to attend. By joining this all-day event, Katie was able to meet the DPEs, many of whom owned flight schools. She was able to do important networking as well as gain insight into what examiners would look for when her students were preparing for practical exams. She added this training to her resume. This training cost her only the price of fuel to drive 50 miles to the FSDO office and her time for the course.

Like most new pilots, Katie was excited to list her hours flown in a CRJ flight simulator, and that's fine, but most prospective employers look for a resume that reflects experience in aircraft similar to their fleet. To be more attractive to flight school managers, Katie revised her resume to feature the hours flown in typical training aircraft. She also listed her experience with a flight-training device, online training courses, and flight-planning software.

These days, experience in cockpit technology is every bit as important as experience in the airframe. Katie added a section on her resume to feature avionics such as the KLN and GNS units. She also listed separate line items reflecting her experience with autopilots, electronic charts and TKS. Her resume was filling in nicely. It reflected a well-rounded, work-ready, aviation professional!

Katie had many out-of-cockpit skills that were noteworthy. She added her knowledge of computer operating systems, application software, web design, podcasting, and social media that would make Katie useful to a flight school when the weather was too harsh for flying. I can say from firsthand experience that the chief instructor usually has a pet project or two on the backburner just waiting for a willing assistant to help.

With these tasks completed and added to her resume, we were able to project Katie as an instructor who was proficient, knowledgeable, and above the average.

First contact with a potential boss for Katie was by email. Her original email address was something cutesy left over from school. It did not reflect her full name. Employers aren't quick to open attachments from an unprofessional email address like ShePilot4U@blahoo.com or SaucySally@gmall.com. Her email address was updated to reflect a more professional image.

If a manager were interested, first contact would probably be via telephone. Like most people, Katie had not considered her cell phone to be part of her professional image. We discussed answering her phone with a professional voice and greeting, as if each call was the prelude to an interview. She revised her voicemail message to be more suited to the professional she had become.

I knew that if Katie were lucky enough to land a personal interview, she'd have to be prepared to succeed. Most aviation employers use a pre-employment exam to verify an applicant's knowledge. Because it had been a while since she'd looked at FAA test bank questions, she boned up with free online private, instrument, and commercial test preps. In anticipation of an oral exam, she rehearsed by recording herself as she practiced teaching maneuvers during ground lessons with a student. She then listened to herself. Listening to a recording is better than practice teaching on friends, who are usually too nice to say if your monotone voice is boring or your style is uninspiring. By now, you know good instruction when you hear it and you'll know if you have the right delivery and content.

Katie would need to have her references available during the interview. She had printed materials, so she filed her lesson plans, current PTS books, FAR/AIM and FAA handbooks in a bag with rollers to carry the load. She was a tiny woman; the roller bag allowed her to bring heavy books and files with her so she could access any needed resources during her interview. She would also appear professional while doing it—and it saved her back.

Katie is the star of this story. She did all the work. She only needed me to show her the way. There's nothing particularly noteworthy about the items she chose to revise. We could have chosen from hundreds. What she specifically did was not important, but going the extra mile to become work-ready caught the eye of at least one flight school manager.

When everything finally came together for her, Katie measured her success by landing a flying job that spring, at an hourly pay that was better than average. For me, success was in steering her away from what would have been a lifelong mindset of just passing the test. More important was knowing that she would pass these values on to her students.

...

At first glance, this may appear to be a story about resume writing. It's not. It's about how, during her resume rewrite, Katie transitioned from possessing a flight instructor certificate to *becoming* an instructor. She went from earning a piece of paper to earning the respect of peers. She revised her mindset away from the minimum required to pass a test to the expectations of employers and other industry professionals with whom she would work.

Aviation, from the bottom to the very top, is a people industry. Chances are that whoever is looking to hire you for a flying job was, at one time or another, a flight instructor. Aviation managers at all levels feel a responsibility of stewardship for our industry; to grow grassroots aviation; and to keep general aviation strong. It doesn't matter if you plan to instruct for months, years, or decades; the industry appreciates and hires those who are willing to help carry the banner. The more work you do on your banner, the more you'll have to chat about after the first handshake during *your* personal interview.

**Read more about these concepts in the** *Aviation Instructor's Handbook:*

Professional development

# Thomas

"I'm OK," the flight instructor said, catching his breath. I hung up the phone, relieved.

I taught each student and instructor to call, as soon as practical, after an incident or accident. The first words I want to hear on that call are that they are OK. When I get that call, I know there is a good chance that the airplane is not OK, and I'm fine with that. Metal is replaceable.

I drove out to the cornfield. The airplane damage was not bad. The instructor had done a wonderful job of sitting her down into the only accessible field. The aircraft owner and instructor walked away without even a scratch. Our flight department's annual flight instructor recurrent training had just paid for itself.

The Piper Warrior had just the week before been returned to service from our maintenance department. Owned in a two-person partnership, one of the owners, Thomas, was enrolled in instrument training at our school. Today, on her post-service maiden flight, our instructor was flying with Thomas when the engine failed without warning.

According to the instructor's statement, the engine had coughed, sputtered and then quit. He completed the restart checklist, including changing fuel tanks. The engine never regained power. It appeared to me that the instructor had done everything by the book.

Still, I had to consider that my business was toast: one way or another, this was coming down as our fault, as either a maintenance deficiency or a procedural one on behalf of the instructor. I braced for full impact and onslaught from the FAA, NTSB, insurance companies, local media, the airport board, and the civil suits to recover damages.

The other owner, the one not involved with training, was particularly troublesome. He had nothing nice to say to me on the phone and often called at home after business hours just to rant. Granted, he was angry that his plane was messed up, but it appeared to me that he wasn't giving credit to our young instructor for saving the life of his partner. Even though the plane would need patching up, it was repairable and would again be airworthy.

The formal investigation was the following day. It was thorough. When summoned into the FBO's meeting room to meet with Thomas and the FAA, I prepared for the worse. The FAA inspector was difficult to read. He spoke only while looking at Thomas. He reported finding no maintenance faults; therefore, the shortcoming must be that of the instructor. *My heart sank.* He assured the owner that the FAA would "throw the book" at the instructor. *What?* He promised the instructor would probably have his certificates, at the very least, suspended. *Yikes!* He pledged to the owner that the instructor's aviation career was over. *My mouth gaped open in shock and horror! How could this be happening when I felt the instructor was a hero?*

I opened my mouth to defend my good and valuable employee when the inspector hushed me. "I'll speak with *you* later." The stoic inspector was curt. I recoiled.

The insensitive inspector continued for several more minutes before declaring the meeting adjourned. He informed Thomas that he'd be on site for another half-hour in case Thomas had any last-minute concerns. After that, the unsympathetic inspector would immediately begin preparing formal, legal complaints against the instructor. *Oh, no!*

I again attempted to get a word in. "Quiet!" He commanded. I thought this very odd. I'd never heard such promises made by the FAA. I'd never been treated with disrespect from the FAA. Flabbergasted, I recalled the many attorneys recently graduated from our flight school and began to consider which I would call first.

Shortly, the FAA inspector called me back into the room. I assumed it was the start of our school's downfall. I was surprised to see Thomas sitting across the table. Thomas immediately took the floor. He said the fault was not the instructor's but that of the other aircraft owner. He told how, after the annual inspection was complete, the other owner had replaced the carpet on the floor and up the side panel. He had removed the fuel selector, then replaced it *incorrectly* after the carpet job was finished. In its erroneous position, fuel drained from the left tank when it indicated "R," and was OFF while indicating "L." With the mix-up in the fuel selector, it was impossible to tell where fuel was draining from or if it was OFF.

Neither Thomas nor the other owner had minded if the school took the fall. They figured we had insurance and wouldn't be too badly hurt while the owners would get a new plane out of the deal. Thomas, however, liked his instructor and couldn't live knowing he was party to having the young man's aviation career ruined. The FAA inspector nodded, snuck a wink at me, and said, "Could you write all of that down for me, please?"

*The inspector knew!* Now I understood why he wanted me in the meeting but didn't want me interfering with his charade to inspire

Thomas to confess. With Thomas confessing, both the instructor and the maintenance department would be relieved from any blame.

That FAA inspector had just saved my bacon!

Thomas and the other owner dissolved their partnership. Thomas finished his instrument rating and joined a partnership on a sharp C182. The instructor aged years in the few hours following the mishap but was wiser for it. He's been working with a major airline for many years now.

...

Many new instructors fear the FAA. They've heard stories about how they lurk around, waiting for the opportunity to pounce on a ramp check. Somehow, new instructors are convinced that the FAA is our enemy in an *us-versus-them* relationship. Nothing could be further from the truth. In fact, most of the operation inspectors are pilots and flight instructors. They've walked in our shoes and they know the ins-and-outs of what goes on behind the scenes in general aviation. Most are very happy to sit and visit if they feel welcome to do so.

It is very important that an instructor have a good working relationship with the local FSDO office inspectors. There are too many times when customer needs require an FAA inspector. If you're an instructor who works hard to do things the right way, you're open to friendly suggestions, and you're showing professionalism, you will have no trouble with the FAA. On the other hand, if you're constantly cutting corners and screwing up, they will be on your back—just as they should be.

It's best to start building a good relationship with the FAA in good times, before they show up with some complaint. One way to start a good relationship with the FSDO operation inspectors is to attend the annual recurrent training for designated pilot examiners (DPEs). Training in my area is free on alternating years. It's a full day. All CFIs are welcome to attend. Call the FSDO before the end of January to get the date and details for training in your area. Another way is by volunteering to be a FAA Safety Team Representative. Visit faasafety.gov to find out more.

**Read more about these concepts in the *Aviation Instructor's Handbook:***

Safety practices and accident prevention

# Jay

The Jay Leno TV Show used to have a segment called *Jay Walking*. The host and his camera crew would take to the streets and ask average passersby simple questions about current events. The answers were so funny and stupid that one would suspect they were staged interviews, but Jay swore that each was real. In Jay Walking style, I present a collection of "Stupid Things Instructors Have Said during a Phone Interview."

If someone sends a resume that strikes my fancy, I'll pick up the phone to speak with them. A resume can only get me so far, so I want to hear them talk. When I call, I am always clear to introduce myself and ask their permission to conduct a phone interview. This makes sure the candidate is able to talk freely, has the time to do so, and is not distracted. I am happy to find a more convenient time, if need be. Still, I have heard the silliest things.

> **Me:** Why do you think you've been unemployed for so long?
>
> **Him:** I don't know, I just hang around the house looking for a job—haven't found nothing.

Really? Did he think he would find a job in the basement...or in the attic, perhaps? I understand what he meant: he was reading job-postings online. I'm not sure how many hours a day are required to do that; however, his answer did nothing to promote him as a professional.

If it's taking longer than you'd like to find a job, get your butt to the airport! Hang out. Soak up the sights and sounds of aviation. Take your laptop and skim job postings in the FBO crew lounge. Better still, jump in and help the FBO's line manager. Offer to help an aircraft owner wash his plane. You'll meet interesting people. You might learn a new skill or you might be invited to ride along on a flight. In any case, its material for a better answer than you would have if you were waiting at home, playing video games.

> **Me:** Are you current?
>
> **Him:** I've been meaning to get current, but I just haven't done it yet.
>
> **Me:** How many hours do you have in the actual clouds?
>
> **Him:** I tried to get in the clouds once, but I haven't done it yet.
>
> **Me:** Are you able to teach GPS approaches?

> **Him:** I wanted to read about GPS, but haven't gotten around to it yet.
>
> **Me:** Can you use a training device, like a simulator?
>
> **Him:** I was going to learn that, but I haven't yet.

So, do you find it just amazing that this guy wasn't hired? I wondered how long it would take him before "getting around" to reporting for work. If I were his client, would my flight training fall behind schedule because of something he'd not done yet? No customer would tolerate that. His failings are so obvious when you see them on paper. It's a shame he never considered what his answers sounded like to a possible future boss.

I realize that you may not have all of the opportunities to do all the things in aviation that you'd like—but first, a flight instructor is a communicator. Try to communicate answers that portray yourself as a professional-in-the-making rather than as an idiot.

> **Me:** Are you current to fly on instruments?
>
> **Him:** I'm not sure.
>
> **Me:** Night?
>
> **Him:** I'm not sure.
>
> **Me:** Do you need to go get your logbook?
>
> **Him:** No.
>
> **Me:** What do you mean you're not sure?
>
> **Him:** Well, you can't expect me to know every regulation just off the top of my head. I don't remember that particular reg.

Let me set the record straight: "Yes," you *are* expected to know regulations off the top of your head, at least most of the common ones. We all need to refer to the good book for an occasional clarification, but you should have the basics on the tip of your tongue, ready to offer to any customer who is paying you to have the answer. As an interviewer, I'm thinking, would I want to pay this guy as my instructor? *Nope.*

> **Me:** Let's pretend that I am sitting across the table from you. Talk to me as if I were your student. I want you to introduce crosswind landings.
>
> **Him:** Uh, I can't, I don't know your runway numbers.

**Me:** Our primary runway is 22.

**Him:** But I still don't know your winds.

**Me:** Pretend the wind is from 180-degrees.

**Him:** ...Uhh... So, what do you want me to say?

I would have accepted just about anything he wanted to offer as an answer. This is not a question with a right or wrong answer; I simply wanted to hear him talk. I wanted to hear some excitement in his voice for teaching. I wanted him to make me excited about crosswind landings. I wanted to know that he could put a couple of sentences together that made sense.

If you are offered a question like this, run with it. Shine! Within limits, it doesn't matter what you say. The interviewer knows you don't have a lesson plan in front of you and they understand it's impromptu. You won't be graded harshly for what you say, I promise. But say something! Say anything that promotes you as a professional communicator.

**Me:** What types of students do you prefer to work with?

**Him:** Well, I don't want to fly with any women.

**Me:** OK.

**Him:** I don't like flying with old people.

**Me:** How old is "old?"

**Him:** Like, over 30 is too old to start learning to fly.

**Me:** OK.

**Him:** I prefer students who don't have money issues.

**Me:** Anything else?

**Him:** Yea, I like students who are smart. I wouldn't like a student who was, you know, a stupid-southern-hick.

*Really?* Keep in mind that he was speaking with *me* on the phone: a female, over 30 years old. The job was in Kentucky and I twang with a southern drawl like Scarlett O'Hara from *Gone with the Wind*. Was he intentionally taunting me? I wanted to laugh aloud. OK, so I'm not going to be one of his students, but he'd still be working with me.

We would all love to work with only those folks we consider to be our contemporaries, in the prime of life, financially independent, and possessing a high intelligence. But then why would someone like that choose to work with this guy?

What kind of students do you like? There was no wrong answer to this question, except the one he chose. How about: "motivated students" or "Those who are passionate about flying" or "I enjoy working with a variety of people." The best answer I ever heard was, "I'm a flight instructor, ma'am, I'll teach anyone eight to eighty!" Him, I hired.

> **Me:** How many students have you recommended for an FAA checkride?
>
> **Him:** None. My students never get finished.

This, my dear readers, was an answer from a flight instructor having 1,100 hours dual given! Perhaps there was more to the story, but he didn't offer it and I didn't ask. Even if we just assume for one moment that there was a perfectly good explanation for why his students "never get finished," is that something that any intelligent job seeker should say to an interviewer?

Perhaps you've been an instructor for the Cirrus Aircraft Company, conducting new-owner training, and your customers aren't recommended for an FAA checkride. Fine—but you completed their training. If you are lucky enough to have a unique and exciting job in aviation, be ready with an explanation that features your interesting talents.

> **Me:** With which syllabus are you most familiar?
>
> **Him:** I don't believe in using a syllabus. Lesson plans are old-style. I think it's better to allow the student to lead the way and to tell me what he's motivated to work on.

This came from a 280-hour CFI with zero dual given who honestly believed this new-fangled, touchy-feely, mumbo-jumbo. My only thought was, "Shame on his instructor and shame on the inspector who certified him!" On top of that, the applicant didn't answer the question, did he? Trust me on this: flight school managers are familiar with every commercially available syllabus. By knowing which syllabus you like and are familiar with, they know a bit more about you. OK, you may not have any dual given and you haven't used a syllabus for teaching, but you were a student and are familiar with the syllabus used in your training. It's fair game to talk about that.

Any professional flight provider uses a syllabus and lesson plans for all the reasons listed in the textbooks and for some that aren't. I couldn't hire him. He would not have a clue about how to meet a customer's expectations in being efficient with their flight training time, energy and money.

> **Me:** What do you like best about flight instructing?
>
> **Him:** Every flight is one flight closer to the airlines!

I get it. One day you want to work for the airlines. However, that's not the job that I have available. Do you want the job that I have? Then be smart enough to make me believe that you will enjoy it and you'll climb out of bed every morning to work hard for my customers. You can still fill out airline applications on your lunch hour and you'll have more hours and work experience when you are invited to that interview.

> **Me:** Can you give me an example of your customer-service experience?
>
> **Him:** I thought this was an instructor job. I don't know anything about customer service.

This response is *so* wrong on so many different levels. No matter what you do in life, customer service is a huge part of it. Flight training, at its core, is all about customer service. As a flight instructor, building personal relationships with students—who also happen to be customers—is the biggest, most important part of your job. If you don't know anything about customer service, then consider a part-time job at McDonald's to learn.

> **Me:** Let's pretend that soon after coming to work here, you need to make a decision. No written procedure exists and the chief instructor is not available. What would you do?
>
> **Him:** I'd discuss it with my student and see what he wanted to do, or I guess I could ask ATC.... (His voice trailed off as if he couldn't think of anything more to say.)

Hmmm, how about asking a more senior flight instructor or another employee who has worked here for a while? Aeronautical decision-making isn't simply a buzzword, and it extends beyond the cockpit to include everything you do at the airport and on the job.

A winning answer would have promoted a high level of safety, would have protected the employer's interests and made the customer happy.

An acceptable answer could have referred to the FARs, if legal guidance was of concern.

> **Me:** If a job offer were given to you, when would you be available to start work?
>
> **Him:** My unemployment runs out in nine weeks. I'd like to take full advantage of my unemployment while I have it.

Am I supposed to be excited about having this guy working with my customers? I'm not being critical of those on assistance, but when you're being asked to report to a new job, there are only two right answers in a new boss's playbook: (1) I can be there as fast as I can pack and drive there, or (2) I agreed to give my current employer notice. I need time to work out my notice, then pack and get there.

No matter how badly they might need you, any new boss will respect you for giving proper notice to an existing employer. You don't have to apologize. Do the right thing. Moreover, be wary of any future employer who tries to sway you from it.

...

As you may have gathered, flight instructors who don't portray professionalism irritate me. Every instructor has a responsibility for stewardship of our industry. Keeping general aviation robust with happy customers can only be accomplished if instructors focus on being, as we say in Kentucky, *Best-of-Breed*. I hope now that you've seen some other people's shortcomings, you will be in a better position to formulate answers that demonstrate your professionalism to prospective customers and employers.

**Read more about these concepts in the *Aviation Instructor's Handbook*:**

Professionalism

Relationships of decision-making models

Training syllabus

# Keith

The airport was buzzing with the sounds of people laughing and learning. WINGS Weekend was a Saturday and Sunday full of aviation fun and camaraderie. To promote the Pilot Proficiency Award Program, hangars of every size and shape transformed into classrooms. Experts and guest speakers were on stage to present safety seminars. The Civil Air Patrol was parking inbound aircraft. All branches of the military were there for recruitment. Colleges set up booths to hand out information. The maintenance department grilled pancakes in the morning and hamburgers for lunch.

At the flight school hung a large whiteboard. It was used to match pilots who had come from all around the region with volunteer flight instructors who'd travelled from around the state and beyond. Keith was a flight instructor who had journeyed from afar to volunteer his time and build hours. I liked him immediately. He was personable and easy to talk with. He was passionate about aviation and excited about starting an aviation career.

My job during WINGS Weekend was to photocopy volunteer instructor's credentials and post enough notes on the board so that a pilot could choose an instructor:

Keith: 24 yrs old, II Class, CFII/MEI, 900 total hrs w/100 MEL

Willing to instruct in owner-provided airplane

As a pilot made an instructor request, the instructor was called to action. Flights departed every two hours with an instructor/pilot team and a WINGS lesson plan. For the most part, things moved efficiently and on schedule.

An enthusiastic Piper Seneca owner chose Keith. The owner was appreciative of an event like WINGS Weekend to help him get current. This was his second day and it appeared he'd been having an enjoyable time attending the many safety seminars. He proudly flashed photos of his newly refurbished airplane for me to admire like other people present photos of grandchildren. Unfortunately, his fun ended when the accident happened. No one was injured, but his gorgeous airplane was destroyed.

Keith had intended it to be a rejected takeoff. With the aircraft nearing flight speed and just at the millisecond preceding liftoff, Keith, without prior notice to the owner, reached for the throttle and retarded one engine to idle. With the other engine still spinning, the physics of asymmetrical thrust took over. The airplane immediately veered sharply to one side. She took out runway lights and a sign when leaving the runway. The runway sign sheared off one gear and she slid partly on her belly, skidding 90 degrees. She separated takeoff flaps from the wing, sending them somersaulting high into the air. Then she came to a stop only after both props chewed through several feet of ground, bending both crankshafts. It was done in the blink of an eye. Neither the owner nor the instructor could possibly have reacted quickly enough.

It was the Seneca's first takeoff, on her first flight, having recently completed a laundry list of refurbishments costing around $250,000. It was the owner's first flight in his newly minted bird. Because the owner had not flown during the months his plane was in maintenance, he was outside of a flight review. Keith was the pilot-in-command—but he didn't know that. They'd not discussed it before takeoff.

Did Keith display professionalism? Was this the act of a professional flight instructor? After all, he did cause a real situation while trying to simulate one—and, he was the pilot-in-command.

Common industry safety protocols dictate that no instructor, no matter the experience, should ever practice any simulated emergency:

- *In an airplane never before flown.* Every airplane has unique idiosyncrasies. An instructor can't know what he doesn't know about an airplane without actually flying it. Simulating an emergency dictates that the instructor allow plenty of margin for the possible unexpected thing to happen. Even a familiar airplane is given a wide berth immediately after substantial repair or refurbishment. My personal SOP is never to fly an airplane at night or in IMC immediately after an inspection. I prefer to handle a possible surprise while having plenty of options.

- *With a pilot that the instructor has never before flown with.* Similar to the plane, an instructor can't predict how a pilot is going to react when nervous or stressed. My personal SOP is to hold off practicing simulated emergencies until I know the pilot will have the correct reactions. We brief the simulation before takeoff: how it will be set up, what he can expect me to do, and how I want him to react. Especially on multi-engine aircraft, I am sure to tell clients, "If the engine fails on takeoff or anytime below 2,000 feet AGL, it's for real. If it fails without us first talking about it, it's real. I never set up a simulated emergency that has a high probability of turning into a real one."

- *On the first takeoff or during the first portion of the flight.* The engines aren't fully up to operating temperatures yet. The pilot doesn't yet have his head in gear and the flight instructor hasn't yet had time to size up the pilot and the plane with the conditions of the day. That's an accident chain made of very thin paper. Simulated emergencies near the end of the flight are a much better idea.

Of course, the aircraft owner's insurance company paid the claim. The insurance protected the aircraft owner against loss. Then the insurance company pursued its right of subrogation against Keith. Subrogation: It's what happens when an insurance company has paid money out because of something you did and now they want their money back—from you.

With every NTSB report you read, there is another side of the story: the aftermath. It's when you land in court to tell your side of the story. It's the point when twelve people (or a judge, or perhaps an arbitrator) is going to decide if you displayed professionalism.

Jurors don't know how much you love to fly and they don't know how hard you worked to earn pilot certificates, nor do they care. They will dissect every action leading up to the accident: Why did you do this? Why did you think that? Did it occur to you to do so-and-so? Did you follow FAA requirements? Did you honor the industry standard? Why didn't you seek the counsel of someone with more experience? Did the victim have a reasonable expectation that you would protect him from harm...and did you?

The airplane owner's insurance company won their case. Keith, at 24 years old, had no tangible assets. However, he was living at home, where he'd returned after graduation. His parents continued to support him. He was probably listed as a dependent on his parents' tax return and as a resident on their homeowners' insurance policy. Long story short: Keith's parents ended up having to pay the money due to the aircraft owner's insurance company for the destruction of the aircraft.

The *Aviation Instructor's Handbook* talks *all around* the subject of professionalism without ever offering a definition or even an accurate description. I'm certainly not going to attempt a definition, but I might suggest a Flight Instructor's Hippocratic Oath:

> To the best of my ability and judgment: I will respect the work of those in whose steps I walk and gladly share my knowledge with those who are to follow. I will remember that there is art as well as science in what I do. I will not be ashamed to say "I don't know," nor will I fail to call upon colleagues when the skills of another might benefit a client.
>
> I will remember that I am a member of society, with special obligations to all my fellow aviators. My actions and decisions must do no harm—not to the student, his ego, his body, his possessions or his pocketbook; not to the airplane, the airport, the other vehicles or structures around; and not to innocent people or the trust of the non-flying public.

How do you accomplish this? By:

- Staying current with knowledge, trends, procedures, and industry standards.

- Being careful and diligent—by doing everything you do with deliberate thoughtfulness and mindfulness.

- Having a discipline for safety any time you're at the airport or around an airplane.

- Being committed to your client's best interests—by managing the client's expectations.

- Adhering to the rules of good business, ethics and common sense.

- Keeping accurate and professional records reflecting the good and valuable work you've done.

- Maintaining high expectations for yourself as a pilot and as an instructor.

- Recognizing that your job is that of a teacher, a leader, and a mentor; setting an example for others to follow.

I have hired a few flight instructors who have never worked *any* job before coming to my school. Trying to teach professionalism to someone who's never seen it in action is like trying to teach trim. It has to be experienced to be understood. If instructing is your first job, then start noticing how professionals treat you. Interview someone you admire and trust to give you advice on becoming a professional.

...

As a side note, The FAA Pilot Proficiency Program is an excellent way for instructors to network with safety experts. It's one means to free or low-cost continuing education and training resources. If you are a professional instructor who cares one iota about safety, then support and participate in *the* largest safety initiative in the industry. If you haven't yet, I strongly suggest that you log on and earn your WINGS.

Both flight instructor associations, NAFI (the National Association of Flight Instructors) and SAFE (the Society of Aviation and Flight

**Read more about these concepts in the *Aviation Instructor's Handbook:***

Professionalism

Professional development

Continuing education

FAA Pilot Proficiency Program

Professional organizations

Educators), and have excellent websites with information about memberships, flight instructor liability, and errors-and-omissions insurance, as well as excellent resources, networking, continuing education opportunities, and mentoring. Don't simply join as a member, but become active in your professional association as another way to demonstrate your intentions at professionalism.

# John

"I'm an Air Force instructor, ma'am, how hard can this be?"

Still in his early 40s, John had separated from the Air Force only two weeks before. He had completed the required equivalency exams so that he came to us having a commercial pilot certificate. Although he was an instructor pilot in the military, he still required an FAA flight instructor certificate. John had an esteemed civilian aviation position waiting for him—just as soon as he obtained a CFI.

We had two weeks to get it done.

Two weeks, just fourteen days, to learn civilian terminology and jargon, to pass two knowledge exams, to become proficient in a piston airplane, and to pass what is arguably the most difficult checkride in general-aviation—and to do it all within weather and the FAA's scheduling restraints. Two weeks to complete a rigorous VA-approved, 141 training syllabus that had no flexibility. "No way it can be done," I declared and cautioned against attempting it.

John enrolled with full knowledge that we would grant him access to our best training resources but that we couldn't be held to his fourteen-day deadline. Despite his wishes, I marked an anticipated graduation for 90 days on the paperwork.

John was highly disciplined. He brought that and every ounce of confidence and intelligence each day to school. He and his instructor were preflighting an aircraft every morning by 0700. They hustled between ground training and flight throughout each day, planning short breaks mid-morning and mid-afternoon. They planned a full hour for lunch, but it was a working lunch and they usually adjourned at 7:00 p.m. John carried a pile of books back to the motel each night for three or four hours of self-study in preparation for the next day. It was rigorous.

After day four, I began to notice deep circles forming beneath John's eyes. By day six, he had clearly lost weight. He was exhausted and he wasn't having fun. He wasn't smiling as he reflected, "How is it that I've been flying all these years and don't know all this stuff?"

Being in the military, John had come from a homogenous group where everyone walked and talked the same, had similar backgrounds and training, and had clearly defined goals for their future. He found it difficult teaching in an environment where students were each so unique and whose motivations were a bit fuzzy. In the military, John had rank and the respect it demanded, but in civilian life, he was expected to adapt to the customers. While some students understood his presence to be that of a strong leader, others perceived it as condescending and intimidating. Communicating with civilians required him to tone down his display of competence and warm up his personality so that students would trust him. It was difficult for him to talk with any depth or understanding about the civilian industry, but John was a fighting man and was determined to make the transformation to a civilian aviator—even if it killed him.

*Time for the chief to step in.*

It's good to have a goal when that goal motivates the student to set priorities and organize time. John's deadline was not working to his advantage. He wasn't eating or sleeping right. His training was not relaxed; he was trying to use brute strength and determination to force material into his brain. Nothing in this training environment was conducive to solid learning. When I suggested that we needed to slow down, John became agitated. He felt it was his decision to make. He was physically and mentally fit to perform under pressure. He said he could "take it," as if it was an endurance test, but the brain doesn't work the same as the body does.

John's flight instructor didn't look much better. He was also feeling the pressure. He liked John and cared about him. He wanted to see John succeed with his important new civilian position. I worried that the instructor would be motivated to take shortcuts to achieve John's deadline.

By the ninth day, John had passed both knowledge exams. They had covered an amazing amount of material. He was performing well in the plane, but he was still a long way off from being checkride-ready. After lunch, I walked into the classroom to find both John and the instructor heads down on the table, fast asleep. I quietly slipped out, closing the door behind.

The ninth day was the day we needed to set an appointment with the FSDO for John's checkride. It was always a balancing act: the FSDO required five days advance notice to schedule a ride. The instructor wasn't always finished with training when we made the appointment. I would usually sign off for making an appointment if training was 98 percent done, but clearly John's checkride wasn't going to happen when he wanted.

Somewhere around 4:00 p.m., they woke up, and they were feisty. The FSDO office would close in 30 minutes and they needed me to sign off for an appointment. I listed all the reasons why we couldn't. John swore that he would make the mark. He handed me his cell phone to make the call. Instead, I suggested that we call his prospective employer and ask for more time to complete training.

To John, meeting his deadline was honoring an obligation he'd made. He'd made a commitment and found it difficult not to keep his word. He had worked hard. He was capable of bearing multiple responsibilities and he wanted the opportunity to succeed. To him, success translated into "just let me *try* the checkride" to see if he could pass. *That's not the way it works.*

I have no doubt that John and his instructor would have moved mountains to make the deadline. With a charming, intelligent, motivated student like John, any instructor would have gone the extra distance for him. If allowed to "try the checkride," we would have set him up for failure. He wasn't close to being ready. Moreover, it would have undermined *everything* we were trying to teach about having standards and the integrity to uphold them; about acting in the best interest of a client; and about looking at success as something beyond the checkride.

Reluctantly, John called his prospective employer and relayed our status. As a military man, he felt the sting of defeat. I told him to blame the delay on the school. "Nonsense," the employer just laughed, "I knew there was no way to get it done in two weeks. Take the time you need. Do it right. The job is yours; we'll hold it for you." Everyone in the room breathed a great sigh of relief.

With the great weight lifted, John was able to relax. As the days passed, the deep circles under his eyes disappeared. He began to enjoy training and interacting with the students. He passed his practical exam, on the first attempt, 29 days after enrollment. Immediately following, he moved into his new position as aviation department head with a prestigious aviation university. He vowed to help students set realistic goals for their training.

...

The best sponge made of the finest material can only absorb water at a certain rate. If you continue to heap water on it at a faster rate than it can absorb, you'll find yourself standing in a sloppy mess. Likewise, the human brain has a limited capacity to learn. It simply takes time to process and file new information. Once training exceeds the brain's ability to absorb, continuing to push beyond its limit is counterproductive.

While individual students differ in how much and how fast they absorb new information, even the most intelligent and motivated student has a limit. John thought he knew where his was.

**Read more about these concepts in the** *Aviation Instructor's Handbook:*

Evaluation of student ability

Human nature and motivation

Factors affecting decision-making and goal setting

# Andrew & Barry

"You both want to learn commercial maneuvers?" I confirmed.

"Yes, and we want to be able to do them to commercial pilot standards."

"But neither of you intend to pursue a commercial certificate?" I continued.

"That's right."

"May I ask what you have in mind?"

Andrew and Barry were fierce competitors. They possessed both mental and physical agility, moving with the flexibility of men half their age and bantering with a quick wit. I liked them both immediately. Apparently, several times each year, they took to the skies to compete for Best Flying Partner. It was their most distinguished title.

They had owned a C182 together for several years and had come to love their playful competitions as a fun way to keep each other's skills polished. They each possessed a private pilot certificate with an instrument rating. The appointment with me this morning was to brainstorm content for a few new contests; they had grown bored with the regular routine. "Anything goes!" they both assured me.

They each had logged nearly 1,000 hours, "...but we don't consider hours all that important," offered Andrew.

"Yeah," added Barry, "Most of my hours were running circles in the traffic pattern. That did little to make me a better pilot. New skills, new knowledge and new experiences are what we want."

Andrew and Barry continued to tease each other. They recalled memorable matches and how one had gotten the better of the other. They were aware of the statistics on loss-of-control-type accidents. They felt that learning commercial maneuvers would keep them proficient in controlling the airplane in a different way than instrument procedures and it would be worthwhile to learn something new. Andrew said, "We want to feel comfortable in a wide range of flying, not just straight-and-level or medium bank turns."

"Yea," Barry added. "I want aircraft control to be so comfortable and intuitive for me that I have a few brain cells left over to deal with the unexpected."

They had done a good job in designing their tournaments. They used WINGS lesson plans as content, but without an instructor, and, according to Andrew, "What we do is scratch out anything that implies plus-or-minus 100 feet. We're way beyond that."

"Yeah," Barry added, "that's for amateurs—or for Andrew if he's having a bad day." As they told it, nothing less than perfect aircraft control, plus-or-minus-zero, would do.

"We seldom achieve it," Andrew shrugged, "but it's a goal." It would be a challenge for me to find ways to improve their ritual.

Their C182 was a classic 1979 model but with an added moving-map GPS and updated autopilot. She also boasted a new Shadin Fuel Analyzer, which was sometimes part of a rivalry in estimating the amount of fuel used. The plane was sparkling clean, including a new shine of buffed wax, which I understood was the prize after the last competition. "Oh yeah, there's gotta be a reason to sweat," said Barry. "We always find some little thing to make winning more interesting. Andrew lost the game last time so he had to wash and wax her."

"Yeah, but as I recall, you had to buy lunch and beer the time before that," Andrew smiled and winked at me. Their playfulness never seemed to end.

There was never a dull minute around those two. I laughed so hard sometimes my mouth hurt. They learned chandelles, lazy eights, commercial steep turns, steep spirals, eights on pylons, and emergency descents. After verifying that we could remain in the utility category, they made a strict rule that if I flew with one, the other sat in the back seat. Each wanted to assure that I taught them both the exact same way so one didn't get an advantage.

In addition to the commercial maneuvers, I suggested they add a basic ground instructor certificate, which would require them to refresh ground school knowledge. I also recommended a cross-country race. Just like the Powder Puff Derby (now called the Air Race Classic), results weren't about time as much as how close each came in estimating their time and fuel. This would require very precise preflight planning and flying.

I loved spending time with Andrew and Barry and thought their playful proficiency was delightful. However, I cautioned them both about carrying it too far. It would be easy for one to over-focus on winning and cross the safety barrier. I warned against peer pressure and mindset. To help them maintain their rivalry at a healthy level, I suggested they attend a NIFA competition. The National Intercollegiate Flying Association hosts competitions on nearly every aspect of general aviation. NIFA could help them set up objective scoring and show them how to engage in competition that was friendly and safe.

One chilly day in January, Andrew and Barry wandered into the flight school looking a little depressed. When I inquired what was wrong, they vocalized their displeasure with the weather and how low ceilings had cancelled their VFR competition and PIREPS for ice prevented an IFR substitute. When I challenged, "Oh no you don't, we'll just move you to the training device," They looked at each other and grinned. I could tell the game was afoot.

I operated the full-motion training device, allowing each to fly while the other scored and watched how I programmed the device for equipment failures and changes in flight conditions. Spending this time with them, watching them go for the gold, inspired me to consider a new idea for staff annual standardization training.

With the help of Andrew and Barry, we designed the *Top Gun Competition* for the school. Ours would start with an oral quiz, followed by a flight assignment conducted in the training device. The president of the school sat as judge. Each instructor started with 100 points and then received deductions for any deviation from perfect. I was proud to be able to show off my staff to the boss.

As a Part 141 school, instructors were required to participate in annual standardization training. I announced the new game in a staff powwow. The *Top Gun Competition* would begin in 30 days. Knowing that flight instructors spend a lot of time in an airplane, but not much time flying, I hoped that a few would use the advance notice to bone up on any maneuvers they didn't often perform. To add a little excitement, I selected a beautiful leather bomber jacket with a sheepskin lining and detachable hood as the prize.

The jacket hung on a hangar, displayed in my office. When an instructor visited, I'd insist he try it on. "Zip it up," I'd offer. "Feel the sheepskin, smell the leather and feel like a Top Gun." I know…it was almost cruel.

Andrew and Barry seemed delighted when I solicited their help. Under their supervision, Top Gun was fun while at the same time motivating everyone to stretch to their best. The competition was a huge hit. The instructors were jabbing each other on individual scores, but in a friendly way. The scores were remarkably close, but Winston was the instructor in last place. He took it in good stride, vowing to do better next year. In his second year, Winston took the first place trophy, a handheld navigational transceiver. Winston's success, I thought, was the perfect reason to continue Top Gun and we had a perpetual plaque designed to hang in the classroom with an annual Top Gun's name inscribed.

Andrew and Barry continued to fly for many more years together. In my opinion, they approached continuing training the way it should be: challenging, regular, with a friend, and fun.

...

Most of the time spent in pilot training focuses only on what is needed to pass the test, and most proficiency training reviews the same items. Training for the test does little to prepare us for the *real* test—that which comes after the examiner has signed a temporary certificate. The real test is being confident and competent in a variety of situations. It's being comfortable enough to enjoy our new sport and hobby. That's why it's important to continue growing as a pilot: to plan continuing training, after certification, that takes us beyond where we currently are so that we have new experiences and skills. Whether you are designing a training program for yourself or for a client, plan training that stretches so that each flight adds a new experience.

**Read more about these concepts in the** *Aviation Instructor's Handbook:*

Standards of performance

Emphasizing the positive

Safety practices and accident prevention

Professional development

# Jason

The instructor was apologetic. "I'm sorry, we can't fly your airplane without the necessary papers." Jason, the customer was embarrassed. The flight into KLEX had been conducted without the required paperwork on board.

He'd flown the multi-engine Seneca to KLEX for a multi-day recurrent training program. However, when the instructor surveyed the pertinent papers, he found the weight-and-balance missing. The owner couldn't produce any official record of basic empty weight or moment, nor were there any calculations endorsed by a maintenance technician. Jason called the tech who agreed to email a scan of the necessary paperwork.

The instructor personally performed a thorough preflight inspection before his first flight in an unfamiliar airplane. He was on the lookout for a cockpit having numerous INOP stickers on the panel indicating an unacceptable level of deferred maintenance. He was also listening to the owner, vigilant to hear any mention about possible INOP equipment *without* a sticker, indicating the owner may not *know* about the proper way to defer maintenance. Few airplanes are in 100-percent tip-top shape, but we didn't want our instructors having any surprises. Jason's Seneca appeared to have everything in good working order.

In reviewing the aircraft's maintenance logs, it was obvious that this owner took exceptional care of his aircraft. Inspections were performed exactly on time with regular oil changes about six months after the annual. The last inspection had included a massive amount of work. The instructor searched for those very special and required words, "Returned to Service." Without an authorization for return to service, the inspection may have been performed but not completed, or it may have been completed but not met standards. The authority to return to service is the most important aspect for an instructor to see. It's usually the last sentence in the entry.

Our course allowed a three-hour block of time to work on anything of the pilot's choosing. When asked how he'd like to spend that time, Jason said, "I've never been able to land this plane the way I would like to. If you could fix my landings it would be great." Despite being an accomplished pilot, he had a few hair-raising examples of horrid landings he'd made since flying this Seneca.

Soon after, the instructor received the needed information from the tech. Everything seemed to be in order. However, when the instructor asked Jason to calculate a weight and balance for their flight, Jason couldn't get the numbers to work. Despite carefully verifying every step, there appeared to be no way for the instructor and owner to fly the Seneca and remain inside the envelope.

The instructor took over. The numbers didn't work for him either. After much bewilderment, the instructor, an expert on Seneca aircraft, felt there must be a typo in the aircraft's basic empty weight. It just seemed off. They called the technician. He confirmed the problem, recalculated, and faxed a new sign off. In the five years that Jason had owned the plane, he had never noticed the mistake in the data.

With that being the problem, the instructor asked, "How did you ever get a weight and balance problem to work for you over the years?" Jason admitted that he had never actually done calculations on his airplane. He always flew with just him and his wife. Because they were never even close to max gross weight, he assumed that everything was OK.

With the corrected data, Jason soon had workable W&B calculations. However, with the two of them in the plane, they required 75 pounds of ballast in the rear baggage compartment to be in balance. This came as a surprise to him. They found the same to be true when the calculations were performed using his wife's weight. For all these years, Jason had been flying his Seneca well outside of the CG limit.

The scary part is that if the instructor had failed to survey the pertinent papers, they would have flown the plane. They would have been practicing maneuvers with a CG way outside the forward limit.

After the first flight, Jason was thrilled with his landing and gave all the credit for his newly perfected technique to the instructor. That is, until the instructor told him how much easier any airplane lands when it's within CG limits. Jason got his wish. The instructor had fixed his landings.

···

Before flying any customer-provided aircraft, our training SOP required the instructor to lay hands on each document; to know the status of each required inspection, recurring ADs, and inoperative equipment; and to review the overall condition of the aircraft.

Surveying aircraft airworthiness marks you as a careful, thorough, diligent flight instructor who complies with regulations and other rules of safety. It sets the stage for a customer to feel safe and secure while in your care and under your guidance. It's good risk management. It's a part of the PAVE and 5Ps Checklists. It's an accident prevention practice and the mark of a professional.

Logbook entries are important even for a familiar aircraft. It's uncanny how an airplane knows when it's Friday afternoon. There's some unwritten rule that an airplane is required to have something mechanical go wrong on Friday afternoon to ensure that the maintenance shop is in a frenzy to return the aircraft to service in time for weekend flying. Oftentimes, the techs will push the airplane from the hangar right at the stroke of 5:00 p.m. and waive off with a, "If it's OK, I'll get you the paperwork first thing on Monday." No, it's not OK! You need that work properly signed off before flight.

Even within our own training fleet, instructors paid particular attention to ADs that were recurring, coinciding with "the next regularly scheduled inspection." For instance, there is a recurring seat track AD on the C172. A 100-hour inspection has a 10-hour grace period, but the reoccurring AD does not. There is no grace period on an AD. If the 100-hour is the next regularly scheduled inspection, and the AD is not done on the 100-hour mark, the pilot-in-command can be cited for over-flying the AD.

We applied the same training SOPs to all owner-provided aircraft, including the student pilot who purchased a C152 and hired us to teach him to fly in his plane, and the pilot who presented with his C172 for a flight review. These are particularly concerning scenarios for airworthiness as the instructor might be the pilot-in-command.

The owner/operator is responsible for having repairs done, but it is the pilot-in-command who is responsible for ensuring that inspections, AD compliance, and repairs are documented before flight. Therefore, no instructor can afford to ass/u/me airworthiness. Unfortunately, many instructors don't even know the definition of airworthiness or where to find it. Do you?

**Read more about these concepts in the** *Aviation Instructor's Handbook:*

IMSAFE Checklist

The PAVE Checklist

# Oscar

It was a lonesome place. Only the rotating beacon cut the blackness. Somewhere in the far-off distance, a dog barked, but otherwise nothing stirred. It was just too hot. It was June and even with the time being north of midnight, it was still a stifling 98 hot-and-humid degrees. Oscar asked, "I don't have a cell phone signal. You?"

I raised my Android toward the sky hoping for the best: "Nope."

The lesson objective had been for Oscar and me to complete his ten night landings. Logging nighttime in June meant an 11:30 p.m. take-off. The main tire on the Cirrus had blown sometime after our third landing. It was when we taxied back to the end of the runway and were maneuvering into position for takeoff that we discovered something hor-ribly wrong. Upon inspection, we found the tire, flat as a pancake. The disabled plane sat at the end of the displaced threshold on Runway 29.

The Cynthiana Airport is only 25 miles north of Lexington, but it's well off the beaten path. I fired up the iPad but found no Internet service. I couldn't send an email to the flight school to inform anyone of our problem. The KLEX ATC had already closed for the night. We found no local air traffic to communicate with, in hopes of finding a friend to stop for us. Our attempts to hail FSS and Center went unan-swered, ending our chance that they might make a phone call for us. We didn't attempt to communicate over 121.5. I didn't view this as an emergency.

"I think we should walk to the FBO building. They are closed, but there might be a payphone. If not, there's a town about three miles up the road. You up to walking that far?" I was concerned for Oscar being overweight, out of shape, and a heavy smoker. Even in the black of night, I could see he was already perspiring heavily.

"I haven't walked a mile in several years," he confessed.

"Well, this is a 4,000-foot runway so it's almost a mile just to the FBO. Would you rather wait in the plane?"

"Oh, no," he was insistent, "I'm coming with you."

If we were going to abandon the plane after dark, I thought safe-ty dictated we maneuver it off the runway. With one main tire flat, it was a squirrely job. It ended up sitting a little crooked in the grass, but an approaching plane would not mistake it as departing traffic. With the task complete, Oscar was huffing big, heavy breaths. I grabbed my backpack but dumped out the flying gear on the baggage area floor. I saw no reason to carry fuel checkers, checklists, and headsets, but thought we might need its other contents.

In the heat and humidity, after the physical effort of pushing the plane plus the hike to the FBO, Oscar was in bad shape. His shirt stuck to his belly in perspiration and his face was pale. I feared he might keel over at any minute. We found a picnic table, and I left Oscar sitting on the bench while I searched for a payphone. There was none. In addition, the FBO manager had dutifully locked every building. With no cell coverage, no Internet, no pay phone, no one around, and no one to rise on the radio, we had no way to communicate with anyone. We were alone and on our own.

In looking around, I happened to find a commercial water spigot on the side of the building, but it required a sill cock key to open it. No problem. Got that covered. At least we would have all the water we needed in this heat.

I was not comfortable encouraging Oscar to hike to town, given his physical condition. Neither did I want to separate our team. We would have to wait here until morning. I discussed my thoughts with Oscar. He nodded, seeming relieved.

Thanks to the iPad, my flight bag no longer carried a horde of charts, so this extra space stored convenience gear. In addition to teaching "survival gear," I also teach the benefits of "convenience gear," and Oscar was about to get his lesson, first-hand. We inventoried the contents of the flight bag, spreading everything across the picnic table:

- Several packets of water, a water filter, water purification tablets, a sill cock key, zip lock freezer bags, and a stainless steel cup.

- A handful of protein bars, a mini fishing kit, aluminum foil, and toilet paper.

- An LED headlamp, extra batteries, chem light sticks, a mirror, and a combined whistle/thermometer/compass/magnifying glass.

- A BIC lighter, matches, and a fire starter.

- Emergency sleeping bags, several extra-large contractor trash bags to use as shelter, hooded ponchos, bandanas, mosquito head nets, and hand and foot warmers.

- A first aid kit, insect repellant, lip balm, sunscreen and large safety pins.

- Duct tape, zip ties, a multi-purpose tool, knife, small saw, safety wire, a pair of leather work gloves, and paracord.

- A list of bag contents and instructions on various uses for different types of situations.

I dumped some electrolyte powder from the first aid kit into water. We quickly consumed all the water packets from the bag and filled the ziplock bags with fresh water from the building. A chem light gave us illumination throughout the night. I moistened a bandana and offered it to Oscar to rub over his face and neck to cool him. After a while, he looked like he was feeling better.

Once he was feeling well enough to laugh and joke, I started explaining my "other flying gear," as he called it. He was amazed at how much capability came from such a small, lightweight package. Most were routine household items. I purchased the outdoor supplies at Walmart. Our situation didn't amount to an emergency nor were we in survival mode. It was more like an unplanned camping trip, but having a few of these items made it more bearable to get through a hot and sticky night.

Knowing that ATC started operations at 6:00 a.m., I woke early, hiked back to the plane, and raised them on the radio. They made a relay phone call to the flight school to start our rescue. After a cool shower, good meal, and fresh clothes, we were as good as new. Oscar and I met at Walmart later that same day to pack his flight bag for any future unexpected event.

...

As pilots, we think ahead and prepare for the unexpected. As professional flight instructors, we have an even higher responsibility: to keep our clients safe and to teach them how to care for themselves.

This is not a lesson in safety; it's a lesson in preparedness. Normally when pilots think of such gear they imagine a crash-landing in high mountains, but circumstances closer to home are more likely. Something as simple as a flat tire on a sleepy-town runway late at night can turn you into a castaway. Stick a few convenience items in your pocket to establish yourself as a professional who is prepared to care for a client wherever you may find yourself.

**Read more about these concepts in the *Aviation Instructor's Handbook:***

Aviation instructor responsibilities

Flight instructor responsibilities

# 8

## stories about
## techniques of flight instruction

Pilot training encompasses a wide spectrum of individuals. *Techniques of Flight Instruction* is a chapter dedicated to equipping an instructor's toolbox with a wide variety of strategies and methods to interact with a broad range of characters.

The stories that follow are indicative of methodologies that I've used to meet individual student needs.

**1** Use a tape recorder and/or video camera to rehearse preflight briefings until delivery is polished.

**2** Find a mentor to provide a second opinion on how well a student is performing during critical phases of flight training (such as a first solo) for the first few PTs.

**3** Encourage a high standard of performance.

**4** Just because it's legal, doesn't make it safe. Maintain a high level of supervision of PT operations.

**5** Develop a safety-culture environment.

**6** Assign organized, specific, appropriate homework after each flight session.

**7** Use all available tools to supplement teaching and assignments: online sources, seminars, flight simulators, etc.

**8** Know the background, credentials, security issues, medications, etc., of the student before climbing into the cockpit with him or her.

**9** Thoroughly and carefully document all training events as though the National Transportation Safety Board (NTSB) were going to read them.

**10** Postflight debriefing after an FAA checkride is an excellent opportunity for additional learning.

**11** Encourage students to revisit personal minimums when their flight environment, season, aircraft, etc. changes.

**12** Include a review of NTSB accident reports during advanced instructional activity.

**Figure 8-1.** Teaching tips from veteran flight instructors. (FAA)

# Flight Camp

Three youngsters and an instructor climbed aboard a C172. The kids were small enough that there was never a problem with weight. However, because they were so small, none of them could see over the instrument panel. Required cockpit equipment included numerous cushions, pillows, stadium-seats, phonebooks, and anything else we could pile in and strap down to provide additional seat height for the tykes.

It's called "ACE Camp"—Aviation Career Education. It's an FAA program introducing children to aviation. I thought it was a good idea and decided to launch it at our airport.

Our camp was two days of exploring everything aviation for kids ages eight to fourteen. A new camp began each week in bumpy June, hot July, and humid August. Each concluded with a flight and the child's logbook endorsed by an instructor.

The route on each camp flight was triangular: three, twenty-minute legs to nearby airports. The instructor would land, taxi to the ramp, and shutdown. The kids got out and ran around the airplane to switch seats, in aviation-style musical chairs. Back on board, everyone fastened seatbelts and flew away to the next destination. In this way, each child had the opportunity to be "the Captain" and "the Navigator" as well as having one leg to enjoy the view and watch the others work. At least, that was the plan.

Reality was somewhat different. After each stop, the kids disembarked and debris littered the ramp as a frantic instructor attempted to rearrange mountains of mismatched cushions and pillows in the correct seat according to each child's need. It had the appearance of a comic routine for anyone watching. But the kids loved it.

In flight, our mini-captains were fearless. Their minuscule fingers encircled the flight controls to command what was, to them, an oversized video game. If not for the instructor, daredevil dogfighting would have ensued, tossing the plane acrobatically across airways.

To prevent these daring attacks, the instructor would buffer the flight control. Buffering involved making a loose "C" with the instructor's thumb and fingers around the yoke. As the child yanked and banked, the control wheel was limited in its movement to within the space of the instructor's "C." As the instructor felt the control wheel bump against his "C," he could instruct the mini-captain in what to do. The instructor could further restrict the antics of our adventurous campers by reducing the size of the "C." It was a great training ground for new instructors in how to allow a tenderfoot to fly.

In its second year, the program grew so that flights departed every two hours, all day long. The after-lunch group was almost defenseless against bouts of airsickness. Instructors became disenchanted flying camp kids after a few retching episodes. The kids couldn't help it. They bounced in the thick air, their tiny bellies full of pizza and pop.

On a good day, instructors deployed sick-sacs just in time. Even so, after the first cookie toss, that smell—it wafted through the close cockpit. Chain-reactions quickly followed. For those whose fresh-pizza-spew missed the sick-sac...well, you don't even want to imagine.

Back at the flight school, instructors were comparing Olympic puke-stories. One instructor begged, "Please don't start a camp for senior citizens...I don't think I could search for false teeth in a used sick bag." I feared my newest program would abruptly end if I couldn't resolve this.

After several failed attempts, we finally saw success after one small change: We cancelled "the Navigator" position. That way, kids didn't have their heads down, reading a chart during flight. Instead, we located several splashy landmarks—way out, in the far-off distance. Everyone was busy and having fun, scanning the horizon to locate a red barn, a crop circle, a water tower, downtown high-rises, or a power plant. It didn't matter what the landmark was. What did matter was that keeping their eyes on the horizon proved to prevent youthful hurling, and flights were again landing with smiling faces!

...

Learning to prevent airsickness is an important skill for any instructor to have. It's the first step in meeting the basic physiological needs of our students and maximizing everyone's enjoyment, including the instructor's.

Let's talk more about the "Proper Exchange of Flight Controls." According to the *Aviation Instructor's Handbook*, "It is the recommended procedure...between pilots." However, in my opinion, it's not appropriate when flying with a novice or with kamikaze-kids.

There should never be any doubt as to who is flying the aircraft. However, I have a problem with the way training manuals describe it. A new instructor could mistakenly believe that they must remove themselves from the controls, allowing a rank-amateur to control the airplane. Then when the student pilot makes a mistake, he scares himself, and the instructor is forced to take the controls away. We see it most often when the student pilot is learning to flare for landing. Nothing strikes down a student's confidence like having an instructor jerk the controls out of his hand and shout, "I've got it!"

It's like learning to ride a bike without first using training wheels.

There is a difference between the transfer of control of the airplane and the transfer of the flight controls. As an instructor, you never relinquish control of the plane. You are the pilot-in-command and must always be in control—but there does come a point when you are not manipulating the flight controls.

If the student is flying, then they should feel that they are in control, but also that the instructor is right behind them. That's the benefit of having the instructor's handy "C." It allows the student pilot to be fully in control, but only to the extent that the instructor allows it. Moreover, it helps the student to feel safe and secure.

During an instructor demonstration, the optimal learning experience is with the student invited to keep a hand (and their feet) lightly on the controls, to feel *how much* the instructor is moving the controls to affect the maneuver. Then, the student is allowed to practice, influencing the plane fully, with the instructor bracketing control movements.

As time goes by, the instructor's self-confidence as a teacher and confidence in the student's skills increases. As the student demonstrates consistency in following the instructor's precise directions, the instructor feels more secure in allowing the student to manipulate the controls without the "C." Only then can the instructor and student be confident with the instructor monitoring and supervising the student alone on the controls.

Occasionally, a situation may develop that requires an instructor to focus on safety of flight without the distraction of supervising a student. In that case, the student must know that when the instructor directs, the student must immediately move their hands to their lap and put their feet flat on the floor.

Personally, I instruct students with a novice preflight briefing:

1. When I want you to take them, I'll say, "You have the flight controls."

2. You acknowledge with, "I have the flight controls," and you take the controls. You will notice that I make a "C" around the yoke to buffer your movements. Think of my "C" as your training wheels.

3. After I see your hand on the control, I'll repeat, "You have the flight controls." Then, you may feel comfortable in practicing.

However:

1. When I want to take the controls, I'll say, "I have the flight controls…" and I'll tell you if you can follow through with me on the controls, or if I need your hands in your lap.

2. You acknowledge with, "You have the flight controls," and confirm to me where your hands will be.

3. After you see that my hand is firmly around the control, you repeat, "You have the flight controls."

It's only with a properly certificated and current pilot, who has agreed to be and act as pilot-in-command, that I use the positive exchange of flight controls as it is described in training manuals.

Now, regarding youth in flight training: One day, one of my male instructors shared his unease about having a 17-year-old female on his schedule, for a late night dual cross-country, and at a time when no one else was in the facility. He was looking at it as a risk management issue. He didn't wish to be in a situation where it might be his word against hers.

Any week in newspapers across the country, you can find a headline regarding the inappropriate action of an adult with a minor. Even if nothing illicit occurs, just the fact that an instructor has to be defended is not a pleasant experience for anyone. It's not just a male instructor with a minor female; there are plenty of headlines having the traditional roles reversed.

As chief instructor, I discussed the matter with one of our customers, an attorney. He helped me to understand the laws and he made suggestions. As a result, we adopted a policy of encouraging parents of a minor student to invite a family member or friend to accompany them on flights when no one else was scheduled to be in the facility. A simple fix supported our flight instructors as professionals.

**Read more about these concepts in the** *Aviation Instructor's Handbook:*

Airsickness

Proper exchange of flight controls

# Stephen

The full moon reflected across the never-ending overcast far below the Baron's cruise altitude. Since 6:00 a.m., the family had been busy sunning and swimming on the beach, soaking up every minute on the last day of vacation. Then it was a quick dinner and an hour drive to the airport before departure.

With headwinds, the flight home had been more than three hours. On board were Stephen, his wife, and three teenage kids. The ceilings at KLEX were below VFR; an instrument approach would be necessary. It was cold enough for the possibility of icing—not that the Baron couldn't handle it, but Stephen didn't like ice. It made him nervous, especially with his entire family on board.

Stephen had purchased his Baron twelve years earlier. He liked that she had a full cockpit of updated avionics. He also liked that she was certified for flight into known icing. He'd accumulated 1,500 hours flying her. He was an expert on her every V-speed and cockpit button, and in operating every piece of equipment. He kept her shipshape mechanically and he trained annually, pressing instructors to keep him in top flying form.

Stephen was very nervous about the icing. Leveling off at the initial approach altitude of the IAP, he flipped on the deice and turned off the strobes reflecting off thick, water-soaked clouds. He noted the time: 12:30 a.m.—exactly as he had estimated. The ILS frequency sat in the box. Taking a radar vector turn, he noticed that the slaved HSI didn't agree with the compass. This concerned him.

Stephen began including the magnetic compass in his scan, not trusting the HSI. He noted the disparity between the two. After only a few seconds, he decided that the compass also was erratic and therefore not dependable.

Now, increasingly concerned and agitated about completing the approach given the conditions and unreliable equipment, Stephen chose to stop the descent and abandon the approach. He executed the missed approach and climbed back above the clouds, into the moonshine.

On top, Stephen asked for a wide downwind for vectors back to the airport, rather than a holding clearance. The controller obliged. Stephen reduced power and slowed the airplane; he needed time to analyze the problem. He entrusted flying to his autopilot while he searched for answers. He couldn't find any issue other than that both the HSI and compass had become suddenly unreliable. When he couldn't find the source of the problem, the helpful controller offered a no-gyro approach. Stephen accepted.

With the higher descent rate of the non-precision approach, the Baron slid quickly beneath the cloud bases and into the clear. The airport was "in sight" three miles ahead. Stephen's heart rate reduced to a more normal level; beads of perspiration began to dissipate. Icing Equipment—OFF; Prelanding Checklist—COMPLETE. He then noticed that suddenly all equipment—the compass and HSI—seemed to function correctly. *How did that happen?* He was happy but confused.

At home in bed, sleep escaped him as he mulled details repeatedly in his mind. He needed to get another's perception on the facts. First thing the next morning, as early as he felt it acceptable to do so, Stephen was on the phone to his favorite instructor. He was still mystified by what had happened.

The seasoned instructor listened intently to each fact relayed to him. However, experience had taught the instructor not to take a pilot's recollection on face value. The same mind-set that gets a pilot into trouble initially often colors his perception of reality when retelling the circumstances. The instructor set out systematically to disassemble every piece of data, probing Stephen for any not-before-considered information. The instructor delved into the situation with several questions until he thought he had arrived at what actually happened. Finally, he asked:

"Was the electric windshield deice turned on during the approach?"

"Yes."

"And that's when you started having problems?"

"Yes."

"And, you turned the windshield deice off once clear of clouds?"

"Yes."

"And the problem went away?"

"Yes."

For the instructor, the answer was obvious. In that plane, when the electric windshield deice is on, the compass is erratic. Stephen became angry, "How am I supposed to know that?" The instructor reminded him of the placard on the instrument panel. However, Stephen emphatically insisted that no such placard existed and was certain that the instructor was confusing his Baron with another plane.

Stephen could not buy into the instructor's explanation when, in 12 years of flying his Baron, he knew of no such placard. Finally, the two agreed to meet at the airplane for a personal inspection. Stephen was both horrified and surprised. There it was: the placard, mounted on the face of the compass, in bold, eye-catching style. It was not possible for any pilot to look at the compass *without* seeing the placard.

This story points out how easily the accident chain builds. Stephen had physiological stress in that he was tired. He had physical stress with having his family in possible icing conditions. He suffered from psychological stress in dealing with the perceived equipment failures. It also speaks to how stress affects performance; it narrows the range of perception even to the point that a seasoned aircraft owner may not see a significant placard hanging directly in front of his eyes. It was a single, simple oversight: how the windshield deice affected the compass. Yet it manifested itself into a significant problem as Stephen's near-panicked mind began to perceive larger problems.

While sitting in the plane, the instructor pointed out that Stephen's equipment included a moving map, which would prominently display the approach. Stephen hadn't used it because he failed to trust it. The instructor inquired, "Does it make sense that *all* the equipment in a well-maintained cockpit would suddenly go on the fritz at the same time?"

The pilot's mind had not functioned properly under the stress. There was never any real concern. There was not even any icing—only the fear of the possibility of it. Even his HSI was functioning fine, it was only the difference between its heading and the compass that made it appear unreliable.

Thanks in large part to his good training, Stephen did several things correct that night: He intuitively recognized that three of the four risk elements—pilot, plane and environment—were building an accident chain. He maintained situational awareness and stayed ahead of the aircraft. He had an adequate fuel reserve that allowed him to escape the situation. Climbing to the safety of clear skies, he was able to think clearly and ponder his options. This allowed him to manage his tasks and relieve some of the accumulated stress. He used his autopilot to reduce workload. Immediately, his accident chain was broken and his margin of safety enhanced. Even though he was not able to find a cause for his problem, when he felt prepared, he requested assistance from ATC for the second approach. He trusted the controller as an external resource and took full advantage of the controller's recommendations.

...

Calling on an instructor to help debrief after a worrisome flight is a good idea. After spending time with the instructor, Stephen had a better understanding of what went right, what went wrong, and what he might do differently in the future. The instructor offered several techniques for how he could manage stress, which would allow him to have more brain capacity in reserve to deal with anything unexpected.

If you are the instructor called upon for such a debriefing, try to get at the facts the pilot doesn't offer. Go beyond the obvious. After all, if the pilot had considered them, he wouldn't have had the problem.

**Read more about these concepts in the *Aviation Instructor's Handbook*:**

Accident chain

Stress: physical, physiological, combination, accumulated, affecting performance, managing

Perception

Risk elements

Situational awareness

Fuel reserve

Managing workload

Margin of safety

Resources

Stephen had 12 years and 1,500 hours flying this specific airplane. He was a proficient, recently trained pilot. If this could happen to a pilot of his stature, imagine how easily it could happen to anyone. A different pilot may have had a very different ending to this story.

# Rock

Rock was a very successful businessman. More than half of the businesses on Main Street in his hometown carried his last name on their marquees. People young and old called him "Sir." I would guess that in one way or another, he employed about half of the population in his county.

He owned a sleek Bonanza that he bought factory-new. Then, less than a year later, he replaced the interior because one of the seats was showing some wear. He was proud of his plane and felt that it reflected positively on him, but in short order he was ready to trade up.

His new airplane, a Meridian, was everything Rock wanted in an airplane, including an N-number bearing his initials. She wasn't factory-new, but she was a looker with all the cockpit gadgets and toys. The Meridian was delivered to his hometown airport. Many of the airport patrons were on hand to provide the appropriate oohs and aahs. Rock was proud, feeling like *the man* as he took possession.

When Rock's insurance company required him to have training in his new airplane, he chose our flight school to do the job. Our instructor was on hand to greet Rock's newest airplane. Part of our deal was that the instructor would fly with Rock, in the new Meridian, to return the delivery pilot. The maiden flight would count as part of his initial training.

That's when our problems began.

Without warning, Rock announced that he had invited two friends to accompany them on the maiden flight. The instructor, quickly calculating in his head, estimated weights for himself, Rock, the delivery pilot plus two friends. He knew the addition of two friends put them in an overweight condition. Pulling Rock to the side, the instructor informed him quietly that his friends couldn't go. Rock was not a man who takes "no" for an answer and insisted that his friends be allowed to join them.

The instructor excused himself, ducked quietly into a side office, and using actual weights for empty aircraft and people, found them to be 300 pounds over gross weight. Losing 50 gallons from their fuel supply was not an option. The fuel was needed to fly high overhead a busy

Class B airspace, allowing them to return before dark. Our training SOP stipulated that we never flew the first flight, with a customer we didn't know and in an airplane we didn't know, after dark or in IMC.

The instructor returned to Rock's party, attempting to draw Rock into the side office to see the calculations himself. Instead, Rock's reaction was to sway the instructor to "let it go." Then, building support for himself, Rock openly mocked the instructor's concern to the delivery pilot, in front of the group. The delivery pilot, not wishing to upset his newest buyer, said, "300 pounds overweight—oh, that's no problem for these planes."

The instructor kept his voice low and unthreatening. "I'm not flying that airplane over gross weight. I'll be in the office." He turned and left the small group.

As you can imagine, Rock was very upset at the instructor for embarrassing him in front of the crowd. He was angry that his friends were not permitted to fly with them. Rock didn't hold back his displeasure all through the flight, often criticizing the instructor. It didn't end there. Back home, Rock was sure to tell everyone around town how the instructor had belittled, dishonored, and mistreated him. He felt he'd been treated unfairly and became angry again each time he retold the story.

However, an interesting thing happened when Rock began vocalizing his displeasure to the pilots at the airport. Having a reputation as a professional instructor, none of the pilots were the least bit surprised to hear of the instructor's reaction. Even the maintenance technician said, "He's your instructor...what did you *expect* him to do and say? You hired him to teach you the right way to do things. Did you really imagine anything else?"

The instructor had a reputation for doing things the right way. Most instructors don't think much about building a reputation. If someone says, "Starbucks," what comes to your mind? *The* coffee you most want? Expensive but worth it? Just the mention of their name brings a certain image to your mind. It's their reputation.

Just like Starbucks, your value as an instructor is in your reputation. You must build it. Whatever image you want people to have about you is what you must be consistent in displaying. Your reputation must be so well seated in people's minds that any pilot knows what you stand for... and what you won't stand for.

Through the years, Rock continued to call on the instructor he had come to respect. It wasn't too long before Rock was ready to trade up from his Meridian to an Acrostar. The only instructor he wanted to help him get familiar with his newest plane was the one he had at one time referred to as, "A total pain in the a$$."

We laugh about it now. The instructor's favorite saying was, "I'd rather apologize to the pilot for being a pain in the a$$ than apologize to his widow for not being one."

...

It's difficult for any instructor to stand his ground when being ridiculed in front of a group. It can be difficult to find the words that convey your values without appearing disrespectful to a customer.

If you notice, Rock's instructor said only that *he* would not fly the aircraft over gross weight. He said only what he would do, but he did not preach to Rock what Rock should do. That's the number one characteristic of the anti-authority attitude— they don't like to be told what to do.

If you are lucky enough to instruct in the high-end of general aviation, you'll find people in this neighborhood to be affluent. They have money, prestige and power. They're used to getting what they want. The anti-authority attitude is often on display.

Information written in training manuals about hazardous attitudes is not geared to the instructor or what the instructor should do. The pilot is expected to become aware of their hazardous attitude and memorize an antidote. It's implied that the instructor serves only to remind the pilot of the antidote if a hazardous attitude emerges. Because anti-authority is so prevalent, I believe it's especially important for an aspiring instructor to learn strategies in dealing with it.

In my experience, the anti-authority personality is all about control. They have a need to be in control over everything in their environment. An instructor should be respectful but not get intimidated. Teach but don't preach. Stay humble, low-key, and quiet; let them be the big-man and the loudmouth. Let them have the last word. Don't take any of their comments, complaints, or criticism personally. This is only their attempt to control you.

As the instructor, you have to stay above it all. Lead by example. If you're in the cockpit and they won't listen, don't start an argument. Let any petty stuff—the non-essential, non-safety-related stuff—slide while in the air and find a way to get the plane on the ground. Deal with it, whatever *it* is, on the ground.

If the anti-authority shows itself on the ground, you can simply say, "I'm sorry you feel that way," and walk away. Tell them where you are going and then go to the john or to the water fountain—any place—just give them a minute and some space to calm down.

"I'm sorry you feel that way." Those are great words to use with the anti-authority. You didn't say the client was right...or wrong. You didn't acknowledge or apologize for any shortcomings they assigned to you. More importantly, those words don't raise their level of defensiveness. It doesn't make them feel you are trying to control them, but neither does it allow them to control you.

Here are a few more phrases that work with the anti-authority: *I notice that.... What's important to me is.... I just want to understand where you're coming from.... I'm curious about....* Can you see how these words are low-key and don't take any control away from the anti-authority while still allowing you to get a point across?

Whenever possible, ask for their permission such as, *Will you allow me to...? Will you permit me to...? Are you willing to...? Are you open to hearing my thoughts about this? Are you willing to listen to my point of view, even though it's different from yours?*

You may want to avoid certain phrases with the anti-authority that come across as exercising control over them or telling them what to do. I don't recommend phrases such as: *You must.... You should.... You have to.... You never.... You always....* The anti-authority won't agree with your assessment; these phrases are the basis for another disagreement.

Rock's anti-authority attitude showed itself first as having no respect for weight-and-balance limitations. During the flight, there were other examples of Rock's quick defense mechanisms whenever the instructor seemed to make what Rock felt were unreasonable demands of him. This brings us to another important aspect. How do you deal with a client you've never flown with before and in an airplane you don't know?

Have you ever gotten into a rental car after dark and had trouble figuring something out, such as how to turn on the lights or how to activate the windshield wipers? Now imagine doing that while the car is in motion. More difficult? OK, now add a stranger in the driver's seat—a student driver who's controlling the car while you're trying to figure out how to activate the windshield wipers, and at the same time keep the student driver in the center of his lane. Almost impossible, right? So, why would you put yourself in that situation in an airplane?

You can learn a lot in a single flight. You can see the way a pilot walks and moves around the airplane. Is it with confidence? Is it with complacency? You'll be able to see the pilot's general demeanor in the cockpit and his level of comfort and proficiency in controlling the airplane and operating the installed equipment. Are there signs of defensiveness or anti-authority? You can verify for yourself what equipment on the plane is working properly. Where are the controls for the lights? Even simple things like how the audio panel works and how the GPS cross-fills the MFD, or from which unit #1 NAV receives its information, is difficult for the instructor to figure out while bumping along in nasty clouds at night.

Be honest with yourself. What do you want to be most known for as an instructor? What do you want your reputation to be? Be specific. Narrow it down to a couple of sentences. Once you have the answer, you can begin to display those traits and behaviors to build your reputation.

**Read more about these concepts in the** *Aviation Instructor's Handbook:*

Hazardous attitudes

Hazardous attitudes antidotes

Anti-authority

# stories
## about
## risk management

If I know how a student thinks, then I never have to worry about how he'll react to a situation. If I've shared with him enough of how I think, then he'll be equipped to make decisions the way an experienced instructor would.

As soon as we associate learning risk management to passing a test, we've missed the whole point. The underlying objective is to instill a mindset whereby risk management becomes the natural progression of all aeronautical decision-making. Load the student up with understanding and practical application.

To instill the mindset, you have to exhibit the mindset. There is no other area paramount for the instructor to walk the talk—or maybe I should say, walk the think.

This means you need to show *how* you, as an experienced pilot, make decisions – it happens in the brain, and students can't see your thoughts. Teaching risk management effectively will require you to feature every small decision you take for granted so the student is aware there are decisions to be made. Make your decisions consistent with the student's experience and make it obvious that each is for the right reason.

I start by teaching how I think; it's part of their training and it starts on flight lesson #1. I ask a question, and in the beginning, I answer my own question. Yes, I talk to myself in front of the student!

For example, "Am I comfortable with our flight with these crosswinds? Well, let's see…I've calculated the crosswind component and it's within reason for the airplane. My last flight involving crosswinds was last week. The weather forecast is for wind to decrease but I have plenty of fuel reserve to fly to XYZ airport where the wind is straight down the runway in case I need to bailout. Yes, I'm comfortable with this flight."

In the following stories, you'll see instructors taking the time to discuss important headwork. You'll see how the instructor uses thoughtful questions to draw out the student's thinking and to guide the student's decisions for safe and fun flights. They manage the risks by teaching pilots how to think and how to make decisions appropriate for them.

## Risk Assessment Matrix

| Likelihood | CATASTROPHIC | CRITICAL | MARGINAL | NEGLIGIBLE |
|---|---|---|---|---|
| Probable | High | High | Serious | |
| Occasional | High | Serious | | |
| Remote | Serious | Medium | | Low |
| Improbable | | | | |

**Figure 9-1.** This risk matrix can be used for almost any operation by assigning likelihood and severity.

# Patty

Patty always had a hundred things going on simultaneously. She managed a house full of teenagers, a handful of family pets, a part-time position at her husband's business, and a full array of church fundraising, PTA, and social obligations. How she managed to squeeze several flight lessons a week into her busy schedule always amazed me. Still, she usually appeared for training stylishly put together and organized to the minute.

She was an above-average student and progressed easily in training. There was never any drama or trauma. She just did what needed to be done and everything seemed to click. I could count on Patty to be early for our appointments, preflighted, fueled, and standing at the ready, near the strut. She preferred our preflight discussions outside, near the plane, in the sunshine. Therefore, I was surprised to find her waiting in the classroom.

"Wassup?" I asked. She mentioned something about a challenging tennis match yesterday that had her moving slowly today. I acknowledged her pain and we got down to business.

I noticed her climb into the C172 a little slower than normal and had to chuckle at her obvious discomfort. While getting our taxi clearance, she got a little tongue-tied communicating with ATC. It was not a big deal; she squared it away with them without my intervention. We laughed it off. Before takeoff, I noticed she had not adjusted the trim to neutral. "Did you complete all items on the checklist?" I asked.

"Yes," she said confidently.

"Are you sure? I think you might have forgotten something." Usually she would take the hint and start at the top of the checklist methodically verifying each item. However, when she missed it the second time, I alerted her to the problem.

"Oh, dang it!" was her response.

Sometime after takeoff, I had to remind her to switch over to departure control. That was unusual for her. She also failed to switch the transponder from STBY to ALT. They were little things, but they were starting to accumulate. I began to wonder if the person sitting next to me was really Patty or an impersonator.

In the air, Patty couldn't keep the airplane where she wanted. She was fighting it. Over-trimming caused the plane to porpoise through the air, first 100 feet higher than her intended altitude, then 100 feet too low. She was becoming frustrated and impatient with her growing number of small infractions. After verbally beating up on herself, I knew something was off. This was not her usual, easygoing demeanor.

We weren't able to get any work accomplished. Her day was not going well. I terminated the lesson early and got us pointed back to the airport. She spent the entire flight back apologizing for wasting my time. Clearly, something was off about her, I just couldn't put my finger on it.

While securing the plane, she tripped over the tiedown rope she'd only moments ago attached to the wing tiedown point. Then to make matters worse, she dropped her flight bag when retrieving it from the back seat, sending checklists, charts and notes blowing across the ramp. Back in the classroom, her frustration was evident by her question, "Well, despite the fact that I can't talk, can't walk or fly today, did *anything* go well?"

"Hold on a second, Patty, let's talk." I wasn't going to allow this to slide. Something was wrong and we needed to know what it was. I had her break down the events of her morning leading up to the flight. As it turns out, just before our takeoff, she had decided to take a muscle relaxant, hoping to relieve the pain from a pulled muscle from yesterday's tennis game.

When a student doesn't appear to function as they normally do—when someone who normally does very well suddenly does not—there's usually a reason. I wished I had been more aware of her earlier in the flight and terminated the flight when it was obvious things weren't right. However, I was glad that we spent the time to discuss it or else we would not have discovered the underlying problem.

Patty could feel better now knowing there was a reason why she had not been functional. After debating whether it was safe for her to drive home, we called a neighbor to come fetch her. We spent the remainder of our time discussing medications and their effects on a pilot in flight—not that she needed any convincing at this point.

**Read more about these concepts in the *Aviation Instructor's Handbook:***

IMSAFE

Pilot self-assessment

# Dad

I was born and raised in Kentucky. It was a time and area where girls at a very young age often became pregnant—and sometimes married, too, if their fathers owned a shotgun.

My dad didn't want that for his daughter. Therefore, starting at a very young age, I learned that kissing any boy would immediately turn me into an ugly, face-eating zombie. Even so, for some reason, about the age of 13, I felt the need to risk it. I began dating and Dad was forced to change strategies. The new plan began with a lecture, received on date night before leaving the house. It was always the same.

At first, Dad reeled it off to me. Then, after some time—and continuing until the day I moved out—I stood at attention to recite to him. I wasn't excused until Dad felt I had delivered it with proper conviction and clarity. It went like this:

> I cannot decide whether to have sex with a boy while I'm in the back seat of the car, in the throes of passion. My brain goes to mush and I cannot make good decisions. I must choose if my intent is to have sex before I leave the house. If my choice is

"yes," I must go equipped to protect myself. If the choice is "no," then I must rehearse my answer. Maybe my intent is "no, not yet," or "no, not tonight," or perhaps it's just plain "no." In any case, a no-answer must be clear; it must be strong, decisive and without apology. It should not injure his ego if I intend to keep the boy as a friend. Regardless, I must prepare for my choice before I leave the house.

In his own way, Dad was teaching a young daughter about risk management. He was teaching how to mitigate the risk of becoming pregnant. He was illustrating the art of planning and preparing in advance, to have options.

Dad's commentary was a PAVE checklist. It took into account the pilot (me), the plane (my body on autopilot), the environment (desire and passion), and the external pressure (the boy). He was telling me that the combination of risk factors could not be managed successfully unless I thought about them in advance and planned for them. Moreover, he gave me a tool to "cancel the flight." Dad's remarks taught me a standard operating procedure. He helped me to form a decision-making process to manage my risk.

Dad's story taught situational awareness. By helping me to build an accurate perception of the risk elements, he taught me how to think and act before, during and after a possible backseat frenzy—um, I mean, a flight. He focused on obstacles to maintaining good situational awareness and offered an effective countermeasure.

...

I tell this story because it's a situation that everyone identifies with. Everyone can relate to the decision at hand. Everyone can intuitively understand that the best decision—one that weighs viable options and alternatives—cannot be made while in the moment.

I have used this story many times to awaken sleepy-eyed students in a late-night ground school. Risk management is not an exciting topic but the subject of sex grabs them every time.

The FAA promotes both the PAVE and 3P Checklists. Personally, I promote the PAVE Checklist over the 3P. I like that PAVE is proactive. By teaching the pilot to think ahead, the pilot can equip himself with options before the situation develops. My problem with the 3P checklist is that it requires, as a first step, the pilot to "perceive." In my experience, most new pilots, or even experienced ones in an unfamiliar airplane or environment, aren't able to perceive potential circumstances with accuracy. The 3P checklist puts the pilot in a situation of being reactive instead of proactive. It allows the situation to form rather than mitigates it.

Staying with the philosophy that you can't make the best decision while in the moment, I'd like you to consider now what kind of instructor you want to be. Give it some thought now, so you'll be prepared when the time comes. Where is the line in the sand that you would not cross?

What if your best friend called you late at night, proclaiming he had an early morning departure for a family vacation that he's already paid for. He's just noticed that he's outside of his flight review and needs you to write an endorsement in his logbook. Then, he promises he'll get with you, upon his return, to get it done. Would you record an endorsement for a flight review based on a friend's promise that he'll get it done? What if it were a stranger, someone you don't care about; would you do it then? What if that stranger offered to pay you $100 cash—would you do it then? What if he offered $500?

Don't be naïve about this. We all have our breaking points. Be honest with yourself on where yours are. Knowing what your values are and what you want to project is important. It allows you to build standard operating procedures to support those criteria. As part of your risk management strategy, SOPs can help steer you away from your breaking points.

**Read more about these concepts in the *Aviation Instructor's Handbook:***

Risk management

Mitigating risks

Risk elements

Standard operating procedure

Decision-making process

Perception

Obstacles in maintaining situational awareness

PAVE Checklist

3P Checklist

# Dalton

The dispatcher said that Dalton was upset. He was at the school and wished to see me. He wanted me, as chief, to override a decision made by one of my instructors.

Dalton was a surgeon. His specialty was in developing anti-cancer drug treatments. He was very good at what he did. He often ran experiments that required several hours to develop. Many times, he'd be watching cells under a microscope to see how his new drug affected them. Dalton's unique skills would sometimes require him to serve on multiple teams, including one for prep, another for installing cells into a host, and a third for documentation. Needless to say, Dalton had a crazy-variable and unorthodox work schedule. The flight school team often dealt with last-minute phone calls to revise his training plans.

I joined them at the table. Both Dalton and his instructor sat with arms crossed and determination on their faces. Neither spoke until I asked what was up, and then they both rushed to speak over the top of each other.

While the instructor confirmed that Dalton's solo endorsements were current, Dalton had revealed that he'd not slept in the previous 48 hours. The instructor, considering the IMSAFE checklist and thinking Dalton unsafe to fly, was cancelling his solo flight.

Dalton had called only a few minutes earlier, hoping to enjoy an impromptu solo. He felt the instructor did not understand how his skills were indispensable and how he saved lives. He could only fly whenever a break became available. This was a rare occasion for him. He felt the instructor was unfair.

They looked to me to decide if Dalton would be permitted to solo that day. Handling Dalton—maintaining a valuable customer while preserving his safety—was not going to be easy. He had no respect for the IMSAFE checklist, thinking it didn't apply to him. He justified that his body and brain had adjusted. After many years as an experienced surgeon and scientist, he was fully functional even given little or no sleep.

I changed the solo flight to a dual flight. Neither Dalton nor the instructor were happy about it. Dalton was supplied a fresh instructor and off they went.

A few weeks later a similar situation occurred. An instructor found that Dalton had not slept in the previous 24 hours and had spent most of that time in the lab. The instructor felt that cancelling the solo was prudent. Dalton's plea to me was that this was "better than the last time" and he should be permitted to solo. However, as he and I continued to talk, I found inconsistencies in his story. The number of hours since he'd last slept kept changing. I felt he was being untruthful and confronted him. He admitted he was desperate to use this break to fit in a flight. Except for few short naps, he had not slept in the previous 40 hours.

I cancelled his flight. He stormed out, very unhappy with me. I wasn't sure how to handle Dalton; he was a unique case.

I wasn't punishing him; I was worried about him. I wondered about the larger picture: How can we instill a solid habit in Dalton to make a smart go/no-go decision? I mean, this is his life. This is how he lives, sleep deprived for days at a time. This is not going to change after he becomes a pilot. Him telling me what he thought I wanted to hear wasn't helpful. I needed to know that after graduation, when there wasn't an instructor to restrain him, he would restrict his flying after long bouts without sleep.

The real problem with Dalton was that he had fallen into a couple of operational pitfalls. An operational pitfall is a bad habit as the result of having the wrong priority. (That's my definition. You won't find it in any training manual.) The fact that the pilot has the wrong priority may not be immediately obvious. A pilot might get away with having the wrong priority once or even twice, but eventually it catches up in a nasty way.

How do you fix a bad habit? Replace it with a good one. It's not enough to know that operational pitfalls exist. Instructors must have strategies to inspire a pilot to a better habit, one that is a workable solution for them.

Pilots become comfortable with their bad habits when they have no one to remind them of the correct priorities or what they should be doing differently. What they need from us, as instructors, is to show them where the priorities should lie. It's what we are teaching when we say, "Aviate, Navigate, Communicate." It's an example of a good habit in maintaining the proper priorities.

Dalton and many others I've met have get-there-itis, *whatever* goal "there" may happen to be. Once the goal is set, it's difficult to get them to back down. Informing them that they *can't* do it only awakens their anti-authority and digs their heels in deeper. I find it easier to agree with them. "Ok, I see your goal. We can do that." They begin to relax, and then I hit them with it: "Would you be agreeable to...(a little tweaking?)" It only seems fair that if I agreed with them first, they now agree with me. Agreeing with them and working in a series of baby steps to tweak plans will usually belay their defenses and disarm their anti-authority.

We call it peer pressure, but in the field of medicine, they call it "accepted protocols." When "everyone's doing it," then by definition it is acceptable. In Dalton's case, a 48-hour long work shift was normal and being sleep deprived was acceptable to his peers. He could not understand why I couldn't accept that. I found the only way to combat peer pressure was by pointing out that as a pilot he now had a new set of peers. I made his aviation cohorts the bigger, more important set of colleagues. I made the pilot crowd the group that the scientist wanted to most please. I pointed out to Dalton that in the lab he had a whole team of people working alongside him, whereas in the cockpit it was all on him. That's why in aviation, duty times and proper rest are the norm and are required if he wished to belong with his new friends.

···

As instructors, we would like to fix our customers, to change their thinking away from the Dark Side. It doesn't work like that. Customers will tell us what we want to hear, only to provide themselves with opportunities to do as they please. Or worse, they will find another instructor who will allow them to do what they want. Some instructors mistakenly believe that allowing a customer to do what they want translates into good customer service. To me, that's similar to a mother allowing a child to eat sweets at every meal and calling it good parenting because it's what the child wants.

I'm sure you can remember an individual who you think improved you in some way. Chances are that person inspired you *to change yourself.* Sometimes achieving something significant on the outside requires a small tweak on the inside. You can't change someone else; they have to want to change.

As an instructor, you affect people in ways you don't even realize. Teaching them to yank and bank is only the beginning. In teaching someone to fly, you often change them at their core: their values, their peer group, and their habits. You teach them to view the world from a different perspective. In looking down on their world from 3,000 feet, everything looks smaller. It changes what they determine as important in their life. So while you have them up there, on every flight, inspire them to recall what their priorities should be.

There is no single way to be an inspiration to someone for change, but I believe that leading by example and taking your time to help others to define what's important to them can help.

My mentor used to start instrument ground school by having participants take out a blank piece of paper. He then directed, "On this paper,

**Read more about these concepts in the** *Aviation Instructor's Handbook:*

Anti-authority hazardous attitude

IMSAFE checklist

Operational pitfalls

Get-there-itis

Peer pressure

make a list of everything you are willing to die for, in an airplane. Are you willing to die to get to your kid's soccer game? To get to work on time, Monday morning? Make your list; I'm going for coffee. We'll discuss it when I get back." He left them bewildered. Not a single participant ever wrote a single word on that paper. After their eventual discussion on the point he was making, he wrapped it up with, "I want you to keep this blank piece of paper on your kneeboard as a reminder of your list."

# Ben

He'd hop in the left seat, the right seat, or the back seat to ride along on any airplane taking flight. I first met Ben when he was nine years old. His mother enrolled him into a summer flight camp. As chief instructor, I was happy to see him return several times each year to redeem gift certificates purchased by family as Christmas and birthday gifts. He was at the airport whenever he could sweet-talk his older brother to drive him. Ben was there for monthly safety seminars. He washed airplanes during the summer. His any-excuse-to-be-at-the-airport routine told me the flying bug had bitten this kid and he had it bad.

Ben's dream was to solo on his sixteenth birthday. It was a common request among the younger crowd. Although instructors were sure to log each flight hour for our youth participants, we always began flight training in earnest—that is, to meet FAA requirements—about six months before their sixteenth birthday.

My general SOP was to downplay outwardly the initial solo. I never allowed any student in the school to know in advance the day they would solo. Instructors were under strict orders to follow suit. There are too many internal and external pressures associated with first solo. I would never allow anyone more than a shoulder shrug and a promise of "we'll see" in an attempt to purge the strain.

I didn't want any weight on the flight instructor to solo a student. I didn't want the student pestering the flight instructor about it. My routine line to the student was, "You'll solo only if the winds are calm, the controllers are in a good mood, the plane is shiny enough for good photos, and the all the stars are perfectly aligned!"

Secretly, though, I got excited for every student's first solo and would work like a maniac to fulfill a kid's dream of a sixteenth-birthday solo.

Ben was, by now, a part of our family and I had his birthday marked on my personal calendar as well as on a staff-only page of the school's schedule board.

I had conducted several of Ben's Prog Checks and knew he would have no trouble reaching his dream. In the previous seven years, he had accumulated over 70 logged hours, but had hundreds more observing as a ride-along. He'd flown with every instructor on staff. He'd flown at night and in IMC. He'd flown several times into the other local airports with plenty of landings there. He could navigate all about central Kentucky. He was a whiz with every piece of installed equipment. He'd been for a tour of the tower, a FSS, and a Center Facility. In short, he was well qualified for solo.

A few weeks before Ben's sixteenth birthday, I reminded his mom about the required medical and student pilot certificate. As the days grew nearer, I regularly checked in with his primary instructor to confirm there would be no last-minute surprises. This was the primary instructor's first soloing student so I was supervising him as well as his student. The weather forecast was shaping up to be perfect for a first solo.

We scheduled Ben a very special appointment for that special day, and at a time we knew to be low traffic at the KLEX airport—5 p.m. Everything was set. It appeared that Ben's dream would soon be in his logbook and all over Facebook. But of course, Ben wasn't sure about that.

At 3:45 p.m., Ben's mom called to confirm that the solo would really happen. We had become friends by now and I chatted with her for a while. "Yes, yes, but don't you dare tell him. I don't want him to be disappointed just in case we need to pull the plug for some reason."

"OK dear, of course," she said in her most genteel style and southern accent, "but you *do* know he's expecting it. Surely, you'd have to have a very good reason to pull the plug. It's the perfect day."

She asked how it would happen. I informed her that Ben and the instructor would fly a couple of circuits together in the traffic pattern to make sure Ben was comfortable with the conditions of the day. If the stars aligned, then Ben would taxi back, depositing the instructor at the school's ramp. There, the instructor would slap an endorsement sticker in Ben's logbook. Then, Ben would taxi to the runway to complete three takeoffs and three landings as the pilot-in-command.

"Delightful, dear." She finished by asking for the N-number of the solo plane and requesting that I call her during Ben's solo taxi out. "Yes, I will" I said, "but I assumed that you and his dad would be here, at the airport, so you can congratulate him after he lands."

That's when she dropped the bomb: "Well yes, dear, I'm here now. The caterers are all set up and guests are already arriving."

"What?" I was confused.

"You and the whole staff should come over, too. We have plenty of food."

"Wh...what are you talking about?" I still didn't get it.

"Oh my, you didn't know? I reserved the entire observation deck at the top of the terminal building. We have invited 200 of Ben's closest friends and relatives to witness his solo!"

"WHAT!?!"

"Yes sweetie, and oh, I might have let it slip to Ben that his grand-dad—you know the one who was a pilot in the military, the one who first inspired him to fly—he is coming in from Chicago just to see him. Ben just loves his granddad, you know."

"WWWWHHHHAAATTTT?" I slammed down the phone. Perspiration beaded on my forehead, my heart was racing.

In the world of a chief instructor, this is the worst possible situation: a newly certificated flight instructor with his first soloing student (that's a big day for a new instructor) and a sixteen (just today) year-old kid, having for all his years, dreamt about this day—that's a big load on a kid. Now on top of that, add that mom has invited all his friends and family to watch! In addition, his mentor and hero—his granddad—was making the trip from Chicago for the sole purpose of witnessing the deed. I felt it was too much strain for the instructor and too much for Ben. It was almost too much stress for me.

It was now 4:00 p.m. I hopped in the car and drove to the terminal side of the airport, jogged through the revolving door, and bounded up the stairs, two at a time. A man dressed in a tuxedo and white gloves opened the observation deck door. Beside him was an ornate tripod stand and sign that read "Private Party." *That's different.*

The room was already crowded. A stage and live band took up a large area. They were blowing something upbeat and jazzy, just my style. A large banner hung behind the band: "Congratulations Ben—First Solo." Several people wearing press credentials mingled about. A long table covered in a crisp, white-linen tablecloth bowed under the weight of scrumptious dishes. (I might have grabbed a few shrimp cocktails.) A man dressed in a cummerbund offered a tray of glasses filled with champagne. *This isn't a party for a sixteen-year-old.*

Ben's mom was busy smiling and kissing everyone's cheek. She was the perfect hostess. As I began to notice the age of the guests, I came to think these were not Ben's friends. Not a single one was less than 50 years old. These were her friends. *She's a socialite, showing off her son. This party is all about her.*

I changed direction to search for Ben's dad and found him center stage, surrounded by the mayor and several city council members. After introductions, the mayor asked, "You're going to solo little Ben on his birthday, aren't you?" *Pressure? What pressure?* Feeling second-class, wearing sneakers and jeans among suits and couture, I grabbed dad by the hand and pulled him aside for a private chat. "You have put Ben's solo in jeopardy." Then I stormed out. *I'll let him handle his wife.*

4:30 p.m.—Back at the flight school, instructors were rounded up and shuttled into an emergency powwow. The primary instructor was thankful for the support. Seeing how much the whole thing bothered me, everyone turbocharged the brainstorming. Was there a way to save the day for Ben? How would we ensure that Ben's primary flight instructor would make the decision to not solo if the stars weren't aligned? Could we really pull the plug and squash Ben's dream day? Could we ruin the party knowing the press and City Fathers attended? *Think!*

4:45 p.m.—Ben arrived at the flight school. There was no mistaking that green color in his face. He sprinted directly to the men's room. *It's even worse than I feared.*

4:50 p.m.—The staff agreed that Ben should be included in the powwow. I inquired of him, "Do you know what's going on, over at the terminal building?" He related with detail the guest list, the catering menu, and the presence of his granddad. "How do you feel about that?" I asked. Looking more than a little sick again, his fear was that somehow he would let everyone down after all the money that had been spent; or worse, that the newspaper would be right there to report, close-up, on the crash should he have a problem. Then he was quickly gone again, back to the bathroom. *Oh, boy.*

The staff provided options. The primary instructor discounted all but two and decided the final choice should be Ben's: (1) Postpone solo to another day, or (2) Ben and the instructor could fly to a nearby local airport, do his solo landings there (if the stars had indeed aligned), and then return to KLEX.

5:00 p.m.—Ben chose the second option. He seemed to stand taller, perhaps gaining strength from the group around him. Each instructor was sure to shake Ben's hand or put a hand on his shoulder. Each instructor offered his words of advice and encouragement. *I'm so lucky to have these guys on staff.* Ben was looking a bit better now that a plan was forged and he had support through it.

The primary instructor surveyed Ben's logbook to see, based on previous training, which airport he wanted to conduct the solo flight at. Another instructor pulled out a pre-engineered, abbreviated pre-solo knowledge exam we often used when soloing a student at another airport. Ben had already passed one pre-solo knowledge exam, but it was for KLEX. The abbreviated version was only 10 questions. It covered the specific operations around the Georgetown Airport, where he might solo. He aced it. It was graded, signed, and filed. Meanwhile, another instructor surveyed the aircraft's fuel quantity and oil and cleaned the windshield so that Ben's preflight inspection would not be delayed. *It's nice to have a team.*

5:20 p.m.—My send-off briefing firmly reminded both that the objective was to have a great flight. Solo was not as important as having a memory of a great flight on Ben's birthday. Ben and the instructor taxied away. *Was it enough?*

From across the wide ramp, I could see tiny faces crowding into the observation deck windows. They were cheering and waving. It appeared to be a great party over there while we fretted over here. The plane took off and disappeared out of sight. I could only hope that I had given the primary instructor the support he would need not to solo, if the stars were quirky. *Breathe.*

6:05p.m.—The instructor called to say that Ben was fine. He evidentially lost his greenish tinge as soon as the observation deck was behind him. He was himself again. He flew like a champ and was up soloing. *Relief.*

6:40p.m.—Ben and the instructor landed at KLEX.

After hugs and several slaps on the back, photos were snapped for social media. We all jumped into cars and dashed to join the observation deck gala. There I saw a mom and dad, so proud of their son, and a granddad, who now had a unique bond with his grandson. And of course, there was Ben, who was still wearing that very special, unique, first-solo grin. He played the part of guest of honor with style, retelling the story over and over again about each solo landing. He was soaking up the attention. He never happened to mention that the landings were not at KLEX, where the guests assumed they were.

...

It's easy to preach against the hazards of internal and external pressures. They're not so easy to deal with while they're fist-pounding your gut. The instructor must set the standard and draw the line in the sand. The instructor has to be willing to shoulder the burden if necessary to reduce the student's pain.

Instructors, and even chief instructors, experience pressure too. It's easy to justify caving in. Don't do it. Gather your support group around you. Ask for help. Ask for ideas. Recognize that a coworker may be in trouble and in need of support. Fellow instructors might benefit from working together to find a way out and to relieve the tension.

It's always good to have a few out-of-the-box options that allow things to work out so everyone is happy. What a memorable first solo story Ben will have for the rest of his flying career.

> **Read more about these concepts in the** *Aviation Instructor's Handbook:*
>
> Internal and external pressures

# Peter

Peter stood paralyzed in the cereal aisle of the supermarket. This was his first visit to the United States and his first time inside a grocery superstore. Looking down the long row of endless choices in brightly colored boxes was almost overwhelming. Seeing no brands he was familiar with, he asked, "How do I choose?"

Peter had travelled from Zimbabwe to our school for flight training. He was staying for nine months. I was helping him settle into a small apartment and locate amenities he would need.

He reported that in his country, they had usually three or four choices of cereal in the largest stores and only one choice for milk. "But milk here is just milk, right?" he asked hopefully. When I led Peter to the refrigerated milk section of our store, his mouth fell open. "I just want regular milk." He was becoming impatient and a little angry about having to make decisions—or maybe it was a feeling of inadequacy at being unable to make a choice. Suddenly, he opened the first door in the long refrigerated section and grabbed the first bottle without looking at the label. "This will do," he announced. It was buttermilk. I grabbed a half gallon of whole milk thinking he might appreciate it.

Those of us who grew up in the United States know there is no such thing as "regular milk." Our choices include a wide range of milk. Yet, we are able to discern the best milk for a given purpose. Sometimes we choose based on taste, other times on what is best for our diet, or maybe because a recipe calls for a specific milk product.

A student pilot learning to fly is a bit like Peter in the grocery store, in shock at the vastness of everything and completely unequipped to make even a simple decision. Like Peter, without guidance, they will often make a snap, last-minute decision with no notion that it might be inappropriate.

Our industry has devoted a lot of talk about training to enhance good judgment in pilots. It would be easy to teach decision-making if it were as easy as memorizing terminology. However, teaching students how to make decisions requires opportunities to *practice* making decisions in day-to-day situations.

The first question I asked Peter on our lesson was, "Is the airplane ready for flight?" He knew I expected a full itemization of the fuel load, oil quantity, inspection status, and discrepancies reported by previous pilots, but in the end, it's a "yes" or "no" answer and the decision was his to make.

At the end of the runway before takeoff, the question was, "Are you ready to go?" It got Peter into the habit of thinking and deciding. It forced him to ponder the important aspects of his answer.

Sometimes the answer is not as important as the decision itself. Therefore, when ATC asked, "I can give you 2,500 feet or 4,500 feet, which do you want?" and Peter looked at me expecting an answer, my reply was, "Tell the man which you prefer. You decide." I didn't want to miss any opportunities for a decision not to be mine.

Decision-making is normally taught as a part of risk management. In general aviation, risk management is considered its own thing, separate from knowledge and skill. It's a separate chapter in training manuals and even has its own separate FAA handbook. In my opinion, teaching risk management and decision-making is like parmesan cheese on pasta: "Yes please, sprinkle it all around." It's not a separate side dish.

If I wanted to tell Peter something, I would present it as a question, one that required a decision. When it was obvious to me that the glidepath was too high and a throttle reduction was required, I'd ask, "How's our glidepath?" It might be followed with, "What should we do about it?" If Peter waffled on a decision, I'd offer, "What's the worst that can happen if we make the wrong choice?" and possibly, "Will we have time to change our mind if needed?" Still, the final question was, "What will you do?"

Of course, it was difficult for Peter to fly and think about the glidepath at the same time. Yes, it was difficult for him to ascertain what he should do about glidepath while the plane continued ever closer and lower toward the runway. That's life.

So how can we incorporate the elements of decision-making while introducing knowledge and skills? We have to teach the *why*. And not because it's on the test, but because of that very important reason to know this thing or to have this skill. As an example, I told Peter:

> Thirty minutes of fuel reserve during the day is a legal minimum requirement, but consider that the next airport is about 20 minutes flight time from here. Let's think about what would happen if a pilot blows a tire while landing at KLEX and closes our home airport. We might need to fly to that other airport and land until KLEX re-opens **and** I might like to have the option of doing a possible go-around at the unfamiliar airport. So, for me personally, flying in daylight around KLEX, I use one hour as my reserve. That way I always have the option of flying to an alternate airport should the need arise. I might even want a little more if there are strong headwinds en route to the alternate or if the alternate airport doesn't have fueling. Fuel gives me options and I feel safer when I have lots of options.

Now Peter knew the legal fuel reserve. In addition, he was equipped to make a decision on how much fuel reserve he should carry, not only for our lesson today and not only when flying at KLEX, but anytime he was considering fuel reserves.

Likewise, in my opinion, there should never be a lesson for introducing FARs. Peter learned the appropriate regulations when they were used. He learned regulations pertaining to preflight with the preflight inspection. He learned about maintenance regulations while discussing aircraft discrepancies and inspections. That way he could see the application of an FAR and why it was necessary. In addition, while Peter was learning regulations, we learned a little risk management. I said to Peter:

> Regulations have to be broad enough to apply to all pilots. They are legal considerations and not a benchmark for safety. For an airline transport pilot, the regulation might be too stringent. Given his skills and the equipment he flies, the airline pilot might be safe pressing further—though he may not. That same regulation for a student pilot might be too lenient. The student should add a healthy margin to find an acceptable level of safety. Most of us fall somewhere in between. Depending on the circumstances, our "healthy margin" might be a little or it might need to be much more.

And that's the key: Understanding the variables and then defining our personal minimums accordingly. This requires knowing that conditions change and that the good decision today may not be safe in tomorrow's situation. I said to Peter:

> What's safe for you is not the same as what's safe for me, given my years of experience. What's safe for me when flying a C172 is different from when I fly in the Cirrus because I don't fly that aircraft often. When I fly in Kentucky, I use different weather minimums than when I flew on a two-week vacation to Alaska because I'm not as familiar with the terrain in the upper northwest.

We shouldn't teach or test ADM or risk management as a separate subject. When we do, pilots only memorize the terms. When we teach the *why*, with examples and alternatives, and in the context of actual flight operations, pilots are better able to correlate different uses in varying applications. They are better able to assess the risks and make better decisions. As an example, I tell CFI candidates:

> The FAA gives flight instructors three ways to renew our certificates: a FIRC, a practical exam, and with activity. I prefer to alternate through each option. I like the in-person FIRCs, because they keep me up-to-date on the latest changes in our industry, but the risk is that I might meet someone interesting and get distracted by a good party. I think it's good for instructors to take an occasional practical exam; as an instructor, it assures I still have the right stuff and usually allows me at least a lunch to interview a local DPE, but it's scary to think that I might fail. I like renewing on activity; it assures that my students are successful in graduating and in passing tests.

But depending on weather, I might not have enough to graduate before my deadline. In any event, there is always the online FIRC. I only have to stay up all night and click mindlessly through screens to guarantee a last-minute renewal, but then there is no benefit in a last-minute scramble, for my clients or myself.

...

My master degree thesis, *"Should a Flight School Give Preference to Airplanes Equipped with a Parachute System?"* was published in the FAA's peer-reviewed journal. One question I couldn't resolve in my mind was how would a chute affect a pilot's decision-making process—would a pilot pull the chute instead of using his good judgment and/or skills? Furthermore, if we had chutes, would we *ever* be able to teach pilots good decision-making?

While this paper focused on parachutes, in the back of my mind I was wondering the same about glass cockpits, synthetic vision, and so many other new technologies. I group all this new equipment into the same bucket: It's exciting. I like it, but has it taken initial flight training away from emphasizing basic skills? Are we as an industry prepared to teach judgment in using technology, to top off all that basic flying requires?

I introduced an online survey, and thanks to AOPA's support, more than 1,000 participants completed it. One subset of respondents was of particular interest. Looking only at the flight instructors who had been flying for less than two years, 89 percent answered "no" when asked if they would make in-flight decisions differently while flying an aircraft with a parachute.

The survey then proposed four scenarios: (1) An engine failure, over hostile terrain, (2) a complete electrical failure on a VMC night, cross-country flight, 50 miles from the nearest airport, (3) the structural failure of an aileron, 50 miles from an airport, and (4) an unintentional spin at 1,500 feet AGL. One hundred percent of respondents opted to pull the chute in each of the four scenarios.

Assuming respondents currently flew aircraft without chutes, then; their answers demonstrated that in fact, they would make decisions differently. In addition, many, I'm assuming, made their decisions without having any knowledge about a parachute system.

What does this say about these instructors, and their ability to make good decisions, when they were willing to do so without knowing the facts or discovering the alternatives? Why did they determine it as unacceptable to fly 50 miles and land at night at an airport, under VMC, without an electrical system? Why was it unacceptable to fly 50 miles with an ailing aileron? What are these new instructors demonstrating to the next generation of pilots about making decisions?

Most decisions in aviation don't need to be made with haste. If pilots understand *why* something is important, if they understand the alternatives and *how* to think through problems, then with a little skill and a little self-confidence, the pilot *can* make smart decisions and the flight is very likely to be a boring one.

**Read more about these concepts in the** *Aviation Instructor's Handbook:*

Decision-based objectives

Risk management

# valerie
## a summary

Charlie used to teach an annual instrument ground school. In class, he'd often tell flying stories. Participants loved hearing about mistakes he had made while flying, but they relished hearing the embarrassing ones. One night, one of the members of the class said to him, "Gee, Charlie, you've done a lot of stupid things while flying."

Flash forward two decades, and that class member had now been flying for several years with various airlines. One day he happened to recognize Charlie in some unexpected airport. It was the first time they'd seen each other in 20 years. After shaking hands, the first words out of the class member's mouth were about how he thought of Charlie every time he made a stupid flying mistake. Now that he had some experience, the class member better understood how those things happen and he knew how important it is to share mistakes with others, to save them from doing the same.

I think that's a good story to share to encourage instructors to share their stories. It's not as if you want to tell a story for every simple error, but there are times when a personal example can make a professional point.

However, the *really* interesting story is Valerie. Valerie was a customer at our flight school, earning pilot and ground instructor certificates. However, she was oh so much more. We had developed a close relationship that spanned 20 years. She was a school ambassador, hosting safety seminars as a FAAST rep, participating in Adventure Vacations, managing Kids' ACE Flight Camps, and serving as a travel buddy to aviation events. What I'm really trying to say is that she knew a thing or two about how we functioned as a school and how I think. Therefore, she was an ideal person to help read this manuscript and make recommendations.

It was she who recalled the Charlie story from ground school. She recited the story to me, as it was told to her, 20-something years earlier. She still had clarity in the details. It had obviously stuck with her so that she had remembered it all this time. You just never know which stories will resonate with customers.

That's why I chose to write this book. The fundamentals of instructing are far too important to reduce to a few mnemonics, memorized for passing a test. The real test comes when you have connected with another person, you care about them, and you desire to help them. Will you know how?

# cross reference
## fundamentals
## of instructing
## (FOI) principles

The following cross-reference provides a summary of the lessons learned within each story, for use in building lesson plans and facilitating discussions.

## Chapter 1: Stories about Human Behavior

**Walter** How far? Have a mentor; defense mechanisms; factors that inhibit learning; repression; denial; compensation; projection; rationalization; reaction formation; displacement

**Ricky** CFI afraid of stalls; student emotional reactions; safety and security; Falling Leaf

**Emma** Giggling; anxiety; a second set of eyes; human needs; student emotional reactions; normal reactions to stress

**Henry** Heebie-jeebies; seriously abnormal students; choosing a preferred AME

## Chapter 2: Stories about the Learning Process

**Fatima** Slow learning; low self-image; *the* talk; payment arrangements when a student needs extra time; perceptions; goals and values; self-concept; element of threat

## Chapter 5: Stories about Assessment

**Don** How to fail someone on a Prog Check; general characteristics of an effective assessment

**Megan** No tiedown, no solo; teaching/enforcing self-sufficiency; adequate instruction; learning from error; purpose of assessment; authentic assessment

**Chase** Fraudulent logbook; training records; recordkeeping

## Chapter 6: Stories about Planning Instructional Activity

**Billy** Adventure Vacations; scenario-based training; training syllabus; making learning fun

**Lamar** From 172 to Lance; syllabus design for a pilot moving up; lesson plans; scenario-based training; standard operating procedures; Pilot Proficiency Award Program (WINGS)

**Fred** Rusty pilot; don't forget the family and the fun; syllabus design for an extended flight review; blocks of training; lesson plans; scenario-based training; standard operating procedures; Maslow's hierarchy of needs, computer-assisted training; integrated flight training

**COM/CFI** New syllabus; syllabus tweaking; lesson plans; distinctive training services

## Chapter 7: Stories about Responsibilities and Professionalism

**Joe** Instructor burnout; CFI professionalism; aviation instructor responsibilities; recognizing need for varying approaches to reach different students

**Chris** Most-valuable-player-CFI; good CFI traits; professional development; syllabus

**Daniel** Felon; approaching students as individuals; private client-meeting area; helping students learn; physiological obstacles for flight students

**Clay** The pilot that wasn't; don't make assumptions; maintaining your personal principles; Aviator's Model Code of Conduct; personal minimums; evaluation of student ability

**Cooper** F***; being consistent; breaking a bad habit; transfer of learning; syllabus; ensuring student skill set; evaluation of student ability

**Howard** 709 ride; having high standards; firing a customer; professionalism; providing adequate instruction

**Katie** A work-ready CFI; going beyond the minimum CFI requirements; professional development

**Thomas** FAA inspector saved my bacon; your working relationship with the FAA; safety practices and accident prevention

**Jay** Jay Walking; stupid things CFIs say on short phone interviews; professionalism; relationships of decision-making models; training syllabus

**Keith** CFI WINGS weekend; professionalism; professional development; continuing education; FAA Pilot Proficiency Program; professional organizations; subrogation; liability insurance

**John** Military IP rushing CFI training; too much, too quick; evaluation of student ability; human nature and motivation; factors affecting decision-making and goal setting.

**Andrew & Barry** Proficiency training; standards of performance; emphasizing the positive; safety practices and accident prevention; professional development

**Jason** Weight and balance; maintenance surveys; maintenance documentation; IMSAFE Checklist; PAVE Checklist

**Oscar** Stranded after a late-night flat tire; "convenience gear"; preparedness; aviation instructor responsibilities; flight instructor responsibilities

## Chapter 8: Stories about Techniques of Flight Instruction

**Flight Camp** Airsickness; buffering controls; minors in training; preflight briefing; proper exchange of flight controls

**Stephen** Baron placard; mindset; accident chain; panic; stress; perception; risk elements; situational awareness; fuel reserve; managing workload; margin of safety; resources

**Rock** Over gross; hazardous attitudes; anti-authority; high standards

## Chapter 9: Stories about Risk Management

**Patty** Medication; IMSAFE; pilot self-assessment

**Dad** Backseat passion; PAVE Checklist; 3P Checklist; risk elements and management; mitigating risk; situational awareness; standard operating procedure; decision-making process; perception

**Dalton** Sleep-deprived surgeon; strategies for dealing with operational pitfalls; anti-authority; IMSAFE checklist; get-there-itis; peer pressure

**Ben** First solo party; internal and external pressures

**Peter** Cereal aisle indecision; teaching decision-making; teaching risk management; parachutes

## Summary

**Valerie** Remembering a story about a story